What Your Colleagues Are S

MW00365241

Julie Wilson dares to turn common sense into an actic
book for all educators and parents.

—Seth Godin, Author, *Stop Stealing Dreams*

A refreshing and hopeful perspective on transforming the education system to prepare
students for the demands of an unpredictable, unknown, and complex future. Wilson offers
tools for educators to develop the necessary habits of mind to conquer wide-scale change.

—Elise Foster, Founder and President of Leadership Potential Consulting,
Co-Author of *The Multiplier Effect: Tapping the Genius Inside Our Schools*

Julie Wilson is both a visionary and a pragmatist. Her book is a wonderfully clear and
concise guide for leaders who seek to navigate the road to educational transformation.

—Tony Wagner, Author, *The Global Achievement Gap*
and *Creating Innovators*

If you want to understand what it takes to create innovative and lasting change, then forge
ahead with *The Human Side of Changing Education* and bravely create your own hero's
journey. This is a valuable guide with practical advice and real-life examples to support you
in this very complicated and challenging work.

—Ann Koufman-Frederick, Chief Academic Officer,
LearnLaunch Institute, MAPLE

Julie Wilson's advice is spot on: Find your North Star, embrace the process of change, and
focus on the adults in your system. Every educator needs to not only read this book, but also
commit to the journey of change that Wilson has thoughtfully implored us to take.

—Ken Kay, CEO, EdLeader21, a Network of Battelle for Kids;
Founding President of the Partnership for 21st Century Skills

If everyone working in U.S. K–12 education were to read this book and put even half of
its thinking into practice, we would be well on our way to a far better society. It is timely,
visionary, and relentlessly practical—a rare combination. Discover what our future could
look like if enough of us dare to make it happen.

—Andy Calkins, Director,
Next Generation Learning Challenges at EDUCAUSE

Julie Wilson has emerged as an important thought leader among those seeking to transform
America's outdated, industrial model of education. With this important book, she has
produced an invaluable resource designed to make sense of the myriad initiatives crowding the
educational landscape. Concise, thoughtful, and based on a comprehensive review of the field,
this book will serve as a catalyst for your own thinking, and for your school's transformation.

—Andy Willemsen, Director, River Valley Charter School

Change is really hard . . . and that's on the good days. It can be tempting to give up and just let the wheels of destiny turn, but this book is a call to action. Drawing on proven wisdom, Julie Wilson sets out a path for championing change within the education system.

—Michael Bungay Stanier, Author of *The Coaching Habit* and
Do More Great Work; Senior Partner, Box of Crayons

At long last, Julie Wilson's thinking about how to transform school culture and leader mindsets is now in print for the global education community to consider within their individual school innovation plans. The Center for Transformative Teaching and Learning has greatly benefited from Wilson's onsite workshops and we are grateful to now have her wisdom for immediate reference when she is not available in person.

—Glenn Whitman, Director, The Center for Transformative Teaching and
Learning; Co-Author, *Neuroteach: Brain Science and the Future of Education*

The desire for an evolution in education has reached a fevered pitch over the last few years. Amid this forward momentum, Julie Wilson's book serves as a useful pause button, a reminder that education, at its core, has been and always should be a human-centered enterprise. It is worth noting how useful it is to have someone point out something that, once a light is shone, seems so obvious. I thank Julie—and this book—for being that beacon.

—Chris Jackson, Chief Communications Officer, Big Picture Learning

Where other books focus on the what and why of school change, Julie Wilson's book empowers leaders to deal with the human side of school change. Wilson shares examples, tools, strategies, and resources with schools that are striving to change the paradigm to build schools of the future.

—Bo Adams, Chief Learning and Innovation Officer,
Mount Vernon Presbyterian School; Executive Director,
Mount Vernon Institute for Innovation

I have seen Julie Wilson teach school leaders using the principles she captures here so clearly. This book will offer system-shifting school leaders the practical strategies, skills, dispositions, and tools they need to navigate successfully their journey to modernizing our schools.

—David Monaco, Allen Meyer Family Head of School,
Parish Episcopal School; Founding Partner,
Center for Transformational Leadership

Transforming schools is truly a human endeavor. It requires a community commitment to a new set of student learning outcomes, as well as teachers and leaders willing to give students voice and choice over their own learning. Julie Wilson's book is an essential guide to teachers and leaders ready to take on this challenge.

—Tim Presiado, Chief Operating Officer, New Tech Network

Huge gratitude to Julie Wilson for illuminating such important dimensions of school transformation. The human side of change—leadership, culture, emotions, and process—can make or break any effort to build models of design that better prepare students to thrive in the 21st century. This book provides practical tools and inspiring stories from real practitioners who are leading change. A key read for anyone seeking to build the future of learning.

—Jeff Wetzler, Co-Founder, Transcend Education

Every now and then a book comes out that has the power to not only inspire but to also instill change. Julie Wilson's *The Human Side of Changing Education* is this book. If you are passionate about improving education (and yourself), read this as soon as you can. Weaving commentary from a variety of sources, Wilson masterfully merges research with practice and engages the reader in thoughtful reflections on the changing needs of education. This exceptional book not only asks *why* but gives the reader tools for *how* they can enact change on a personal and organizational level.

—Susan Reinecke, Societal Advancement K–12 Faculty,
Center for Creative Leadership

Julie Wilson's practical insights for bringing the human element into school transformation face major obstacles in a school culture obsessed with data. Nonetheless, her insights deserve attentive reflection and action by every person looking for our children to be seen as flesh and blood learners instead of measurable numbers.

—Jim Bellanca, Executive Director, Illinois Consortium for
21st Century Skills; Co-Editor, *21st Century Skills:
Rethinking How Students Learn*; Senior Fellow, P21

With clarity and grace, Julie Wilson guides educators through the difficult task of unlearning the old habits and lessons of the past to create schools that cultivate the postindustrial skills our students need. She models the innovative thinking and processes required to create the schools our students and society deserve.

—Ethan R. Cancell, Executive Director, Brockton School District;
Assessment, Accountability, Technology & Student Data Research

For educators to facilitate and sustain meaningful school change, they must first embody the change they envision for their students. Julie Wilson's book provides a solid explanation of the change process and practical tools for individuals who seek to not only transform the world of education but transform themselves as well.

—Amy Timmins, Teacher, Lexington, MA

The Human Side of
Changing Education

To:

Rhiana

Clara

Selena

Daisy

Jack

Sophie

Annabel

Arthur

Davin

Teddy

—*may you always believe in, and act upon, the magic of your dreams.*

The Human Side of Changing Education

How to Lead Change With Clarity, Conviction, and Courage

Julie M. Wilson

Foreword by Arthur Levine

CORWIN

A SAGE Publishing Company

FOR INFORMATION:

Corwin

A SAGE Company

2455 Teller Road

Thousand Oaks, California 91320

(800) 233-9936

www.corwin.com

SAGE Publications Ltd.

1 Oliver's Yard

55 City Road

London EC1Y 1SP

United Kingdom

SAGE Publications India Pvt. Ltd.

B 1/I 1 Mohan Cooperative Industrial Area

Mathura Road, New Delhi 110 044

India

SAGE Publications Asia-Pacific Pte. Ltd.

3 Church Street

#10-04 Samsung Hub

Singapore 049483

Publisher: Arnis Burvikovs

Development Editor: Desirée A. Bartlett

Editorial Assistant: Eliza B. Riegert

Production Editor: Melanie Birdsall

Copy Editor: Diane DiMura

Typesetter: C&M Digitals (P) Ltd.

Proofreader: Barbara Coster

Indexer: Molly Hall

Cover Designer: Michael Dubowe

Marketing Manager: Nicole Franks

Printed in Canada

Library of Congress Cataloging-in-Publication Data

Names: Wilson, Julie M., author.

Title: The human side of changing education : how to lead change with clarity, conviction, and courage / Julie M. Wilson ; Foreword by Arthur Levine.

Description: Thousand Oaks, California : Corwin, A SAGE Company, [2018] | Includes bibliographical references and index.

Identifiers: LCCN 2017057549 | ISBN 9781506398532 (pbk. : alk. paper)

Subjects: LCSH: Educational change. | Educational leadership.

Classification: LCC LB2806 .W5445 2018 | DDC 371.207—dc23

LC record available at https://lccn.loc.gov/2017057549

This book is printed on acid-free paper.

19 20 21 22 10 9 8 7 6 5 4 3 2

Contents

Chapter 1

Chapter 2

Chapter 3

Chapter 4

Chapter 5

 Visit the companion website at
www.the-IFL.org/TheHumanSide
for a companion guide and other downloadable resources.

Foreword

Throughout much of my career, when an organization or person in my field was mentioned, the name was usually familiar. Several years ago, I realized this was no longer true. I was hearing more and more new names and they seemed to change daily.

I should not have been surprised. The United States is experiencing profound, continuing, and accelerating demographic, economic, technological, political, and global change as it transitions from a national, analog, industrial economy to a global, digital, information economy. America's education system is experiencing comparable changes.

I wanted to learn more about the emerging education landscape, beyond the flavor du jour. I wanted to see the most promising initiatives and meet the people who were leading them. I wanted to talk with the people who were doing the best thinking about what was coming.

I began going to conferences I hadn't previously attended such as ASU-GSV and SxSW. That wasn't enough. Too much was being written about the future of education; too many new initiatives were under way and too many new leaders were emerging. The churn in players, places, and perspectives was extraordinary. To use a cliché, it was like trying to drink from a fire hose.

I needed a tutor. Seemingly everyone I talked with told me I had to meet Julie Wilson, who had created an independent think and do tank on the future of education and successful change. After a long breakfast, I understood why. Julie's understanding and experience in the current and emerging landscape was wide and deep. She introduced me to key thinkers and doers. She arranged for me to see promising initiatives. She turned each of these conversations and visits into case studies and knitted them together to illuminate the emerging landscape of education and the requirements for success in this environment.

Julie was my teacher and the teacher of many others. We urged her to write a book to share her rich and unique body of knowledge, experience, and wisdom with educators hungry and in desperate need of what Julie gave us. This is that book. I am honored to have been asked to write the foreword.

Julie Wilson's book comes at a time in which America's schools are undergoing a transformation. A nation's education system typically mirrors its times, lagging a bit behind. America's schools were created for an industrial economy. They were modeled on one of the most effective technologies of the nineteenth century, the assembly line, and were very successful for well over a century. Like the assembly line, they are rooted in a fixed process and a fixed schedule over a fixed period of time. On average, students, sorted by age in classes of twenty-five to thirty students, attend school 180 days a year for twelve years. They take four to five major courses a year in secondary school for lengths of time established by the Carnegie Foundation in 1906. The focus of these traditional schools is on teaching, and student progress is based upon seat time—the amount of time spent with a teacher in a classroom.

As America transitions to a global, digital, information economy, there will be commensurate changes to our schools. They can be expected to shift away from the fixed processes and clock of the industrial era toward the fixed outcomes favored by information economies. Accordingly, they will be focused on what students learn rather than what they have been taught. This change is already under way, and its implications for schooling are profound. With a focus on learning, education will become student centered rather than teacher centered. It will be rooted in learning outcomes—the skills and knowledge students are required to master to earn a credential (generally referred to today as competencies, standards, and outcomes). The process for achieving mastery and the amount of time necessary to do so will vary from student to student and from competency to competency for each student. In this system, the time and process of learning will become variable and the outcomes will be fixed.

This shift will render the current time-based academic accounting system—consisting of credit hours, Carnegie units, and seat time—anachronistic. It will be necessary for the education system to develop shared or common definitions of outcomes or competencies.

Psychiatry is an example of a field that accomplished this. With its *Diagnostic and Statistical Manual of Mental Disorders*, psychiatry standardized the language, definitions, and criteria for classifying mental illnesses. Credentialing is likely to evolve in a comparable fashion. Today's degrees are macro-credentials tied to the number of credits or courses students must complete to earn a diploma. A shift to outcomes makes it possible to certify smaller units of knowledge and skills, specific competency areas that students achieve, and to award micro-credentials for mastering them.

Instruction, rooted in outcomes and aided by digital technologies, will become more individualized or personalized. That is, the Internet offers a limitless array of learning materials for students and the possibility of a multiplicity of pedagogical approaches to learning, including self-study; peer-based learning; expert instruction; tutoring; collaborative learning; flipped instruction; simulations and games; online learning; face-to-face instruction; blended, synchronous, and asynchronous instruction; group and individual instruction; and much, much more.

As the focus of education moves to individualized student learning, the course of study for preparing teachers will rely more and more on learning sciences: the knowledge of how an increasingly diverse student population learns. Historically, education has been rooted in philosophy. In the future, biology will gain dominance as our understanding of the brain and how it works advances.

At the same time, the classroom can be expected to expand dramatically— from a walled physical space that typically operates from 8:00 a.m. to 3:00 p.m. weekdays to an unbounded space that embraces both formal and informal learning, which occurs anytime, anyplace, twenty-four hours a day, seven days a week.

Assessment will change as well. Formative assessment will become the dominant mode of evaluation. The education system will continually assess what each learner knows and can do, based upon the outcomes that learner must attain, and then determine the future course of studies the learner should pursue, based upon those assessments. Assessment will be formative until the final assessment, which proves to be summative in finding the learner has achieved the competency and is ready to move on to the next.

In contrast to today's testing regimens, which rely heavily upon examining students at the completion of a class or unit, assessment will be much more like a GPS, determining where students are in their learning and what they need to do to reach the final destination—mastery of a competency. Over time, assessment is likely to be increasingly embedded in instruction.

In such a system, each student would have an individual education plan. Today, these plans are reserved for the growing number of students diagnosed with learning disabilities. *Learning disabled* and *special education* are catch-all terms, applied to students who learn in a manner different from the norm. With advances in learning science, it will be possible to recognize a spectrum of ways in which students learn and offer the most effective methods of instruction associated with those differences.

The jobs of educators will change accordingly. In the emerging schools, teachers will become engineers or designers of student learning, engaging in four primary roles—assessor, diagnostician, prescriptor, and instructor.

Industrial-era and information-age schools represent the poles of a continuum. They are abstractions, pure types that don't exist in the real world. The information-age school is yet to be invented, and the industrial-era school has continued to evolve over time.

America's actual schools range across the continuum, overwhelmingly skewed toward the industrial pole. There are exceptions—schools that have embraced some aspects of the information economy education, such as competency-based education, individualized instruction, simulations and games, hybrid learning, or new forms of assessment.

In the transition, most schools have been placed in an untenable position. The states have required them to maintain both the historic fixed processes and scheduling of the industrial era and to augment them with the fixed outcomes or standards of the information economy. This isn't possible educationally; all three cannot be simultaneously fixed. People learn at different rates, so if fixed outcomes are to be obtained, time must be variable. If time is fixed, then the outcomes will necessarily be variable. The best solution would be accelerating education's transition to the information economy and removing the shackles of industrial-era design that slow it down.

Julie Wilson's book is a gift in this environment. It is essential reading for all educators today, a time that demands they lead change in educational institutions rather than merely managing them. It is a volume that must be read by those who hire educators, who educate educators, who report on education, who fund education, and who make policy or administer policy in education.

Most education reform or change initiatives fail, not because of the quality of the ideas that underlie them, but because of the people who plan, implement, and institutionalize them. In this volume, Julie Wilson offers us a primer on the human dimension of educational change from conception to realization. It is at once practical, motivational, and visionary. I have been waiting for such a book for years and I can't thank Julie Wilson enough for writing it.

—**Arthur Levine**
President, Woodrow Wilson Foundation, Princeton, NJ;
President Emeritus, Teachers College, Columbia University, NY

Acknowledgments

This book would not exist were it not for the help, support, and guidance of many people.

During my graduate study, I had the incredible good fortune of being a student of several leading thinkers and practitioners in learning and human development. These include Eleanor Duckworth, Robert Kegan, David Perkins, and Stone Wiske. Their research and practice into how we learn, and the importance and vitality of a developmental-based approach, provide the foundation for my work.

When it comes to the topic of change and how we, and the organizations in which we work, might do that, the writings of William and Susan Bridges, Ron Heifitz, John Kotter, and Frederick Laloux are the books on my bookshelf with the most underlines and turned down pages.

Thank you to Alison Whitmire, curator of TEDxRockCreekPark, who introduced me to Joseph Campbell's work and the Hero's Journey.

I am indebted to several people who provided me with guidance and support, not only in the writing of this book, but also during the foundational years of the Institute for the Future of Learning (IFL). Heartfelt thanks to Kevin and Dee Colcord, Wendy Everett, Ann Koufman-Frederick, Bob Pearlman, and Tony Wagner, and to Stefanie Archer and Tim Lucas as the founding board members of the IFL.

A huge thank-you to the contributors of the report I wrote on the K–12 Transformational Landscape for Arthur Levine; the report summary turned out to be the spark that prompted the writing of this book: John Bailey, Andy Calkins, Betsy Corcoran, Ted Fujimoto, Greg Gunn, Michael Horn, Cindy Johanson, Grant Lichtman, Pam Moran, Will Richardson, Tom Vander Ark, Audrey Watters, and Bruce Wexler.

This is my first book and writing it was an odyssey. My deepest thanks go to Arthur Levine who suggested I write it in the first place, to Stacy Nelson for her heartfelt coaching and support, and to Nadia Colburn for her keen eye and insightful feedback. Midway through the development of the manuscript, I hit a wall and reached out to several colleagues and friends for candid feedback; their feedback shaped this final version: Bo Adams, Tory Callahan, Alicia Gram, Faron Hollinger, Paul Kim, Ann Koufman-Frederick, Grant Lichtman, Bob Pearlman, Stephanie Rogen, Michael Bungay Stanier, Amy Timmins, and Andy Willemsen. Thanks also to Joel Fruchtman for his much-needed advice and counsel, and to Sherold Barr for her inspiration and guidance.

I was blessed to have this book published by Corwin and had the privilege of working with a superb team. A big thank-you to Arnis Burvikovs and

Desirée Bartlett for their expert editorial direction, to Eliza Riegert for her smooth management of many details pre-production, to Diane DiMura for leading a skillful copyediting process, and to Melanie Birdsall for her wonderful support in guiding and shepherding the final draft toward production.

Several people gave generously of their time during interviews and allowed me to share their story in this book. Thank you to the following heroes who inspire me and others in their work: Natalie Belli, Melissa Corto, Jared Cotton, Zach Eikenberry, Lourenço Garcia, Johnna Maraia, David Miyashiro, Allison Ohle, Lisa Palmieri, Emmy Ryder, and Sandra Trach.

A big thank-you to Heather Martinez and Kelvy Bird for the initial and final illustrations for the book.

On a personal note, I would like to thank my mother and father for raising me to pursue my education, to walk my own path, and for being a steadfast source of unconditional love and support.

The final word of thanks goes to Jay Jungalwala, a man of immense heart, kindness, and spirit. I am blessed to be your partner in love and in life. Thank you for being there for me in the writing of this book and for the adventure of living this life that we share. I am a better person when I am with you.

Publisher's Acknowledgments

Corwin gratefully acknowledges the contributions of the following reviewers:

Ray Boyd, Principal
West Beechboro Independent Primary School
Beechboro, Western Australia

Sister Camille Anne Campbell, President
Mount Carmel Academy
New Orleans, LA

Louis Lim, Vice Principal
Bayview Secondary School
Richmond Hill, Ontario, Canada

Susan E. Schipper, Elementary Teacher
Charles Street School
Palmyra, NJ

About the Author

Julie M. Wilson is a coach and adviser to school leaders, educational institutions, and foundations whose mission is to shape the future of K–12 education. She has over fifteen years' experience building effective learning environments that unlock human potential and enable organizational culture to adapt and grow during times of change.

She is the founder and executive director of the Institute for the Future of Learning, a nonprofit organization dedicated to helping transform the factory model of education. The Institute works with a diverse range of clients including public schools, independent schools, public charter schools, and educational philanthropic organizations.

In addition to helping schools and communities lead sustainable change, Julie highlights great practice and shares reflections on curriculum, pedagogy, and change at www.the-IFL.org. Recent speaking engagements include TEDx, fuse, the Center for Transformational Leadership, and the Science of Teaching and Leadership Academy. Julie graduated from Harvard's Graduate School of Education with a master's degree in technology, innovation, and education, and a bachelor of arts in business administration and French from Queens University in Belfast, Northern Ireland. During her time as a staff member at Harvard, Julie was the recipient of the Harvard Hero award for outstanding contributions to the university.

Connect with Julie via Twitter @juliemargretta or via email: jwilson@the-IFL.org

The Core of Change is Learning

Which is ironic.

Our institutions of learning are slow, some might even say immune, to change.

Introduction

Becoming Agents of Our Own Learning

Before I entered the world of K–12 education, I worked with leaders for fifteen years on how to lead themselves, their teams, and their organizations through change. For nine of those years, I worked at Harvard University, in the Center for Workplace Development. During that time, I was a training and development specialist, career and professional development manager, organization development consultant, and leadership coach. Our department served the learning and development needs of Harvard's 11,000 or so employees and during that time we taught courses on a wide range of topics—topics such as difficult conversations, project management, presentation skills, how to be a coach, how to give feedback, how to build relationships, how to develop your employees, and how to navigate your career. In this capacity, we were helping adults gain the skills that they had not learned earlier in their education. These are the skills that are non-negotiable at work (and I would argue in life as well) and the vast majority of young adults lack these skills upon graduating high school or even college.

I graduated from Queen's University, Belfast, in 1996. Despite the fact that I had a degree in business administration, I was unprepared for the world of work. I had successfully avoided any course at university in which a presentation or group project was required. I was quiet in class, rarely asked a question, and avoided sharing my opinion if it differed with someone else's. I learned (quickly) in my first job out of college that I needed to learn how to give presentations, have difficult conversations, and start sharing my opinion, something I had avoided in my eighteen years of schooling. I spent much of my early to late twenties attending workshops to build these skills and then began teaching them to others. These skills were serving me well in my personal life too.

As I began to teach these skills inside different organizations, I began to realize that much of the work I and my colleagues were doing was helping adults *unlearn* what they learned through an industrial system of education and to help them approach learning in a more fluid, creative, and personalized way. As adults, we are accustomed to the consumption model of education. We often do not question the usefulness of a seventy-slide PowerPoint presentation and its ability, or lack thereof, to generate an engaging learning experience. We are accustomed to the sit-and-get approach to learning—consume, comply, and get on with your real life, outside the classroom, as soon as possible. I wanted to learn more about how to help adults become agents of their own learning and how I could design learning that would be engaging, useful, and tailored to each learner's specific needs.

During my time at the Center for Workplace Development, I was privileged to work with an incredible team of training designers, facilitators, and coaches. The team lived its ethos of development and we were encouraged to dig into our own questions around our work. I became more and more intrigued by how to design a really effective learning environment for adults. During this time, I came across the work of Dave Meier and his book, *The Accelerated Learning Handbook* (2000). Dave's words resonated deeply with me. I laughed out loud when I read how Dave referred to a lengthy PowerPoint presentation as "electronic chloroform." I began to change how I designed my courses and coaching sessions and I could see clients start to take charge of their learning and step out from behind themselves and into their own questions and areas of interest.

I wanted to dig into this more; I wanted to know more about the practical theory of how adults learn and how they change behavior. I wanted to learn how, and if it is even possible, to motivate the unmotivated adult learner. I wanted to learn what the great theorists of learning and development had discovered in their research and how I might apply that to my daily work with adults. I enrolled in the technology, innovation, and education master's program at the Harvard Graduate School of Education in pursuit of answers to those questions.

I felt like a kid in a candy store. I was learning schema, models, and ways of thinking that informed my work with individuals and groups the next day. During that time, a number of disparate threads began to come together: how adults learn, the very personal nature of change and how it relates as much to unlearning as it does to learning, and the power of deep inquiry-based learning and its impact on learner motivation.

Schools That Support Human Development

While I was busy applying what I was learning with adults, something else began to bubble under the surface. Being surrounded by so many "educational reform" conversations, I began to wonder if we had a different education system, might adults be prepared differently for life and for work? Might the adult courses I was teaching, courses like Difficult Conversations, Conflict Management, and Presentation Skills, potentially become redundant if we were to teach these skills sooner?

It was then I stumbled upon David Perkins's (2006) Educating for the Unknown; I did not know it at the time, but that particular course would change the trajectory of my work. The course was grounded in four questions:

1. What's worth learning?
2. How is it best learned?
3. How can we get it taught that way?
4. How do we know it has been learned?

These four questions were a catalytic force. The readings, the class discussions, and the writings all shaped my thinking regarding the need for educational change—not just reform, but transformation. I learned there were schools where this work was already happening: schools where second and third graders were managing conflict in the playground with teacher as guide and facilitator. I learned about high schoolers designing and managing projects in their community and enacting change. I began to understand what is possible from a human development perspective when we rethink, reimagine, and redesign a school to unleash potential, spark curiosity, and invite learners to think for themselves and to take ownership of their learning.

I had originally embarked on this period of study to learn more about how adults learn and change. Unexpectedly, it brought me to a different place. It brought me to the K–12 education system and a clear understanding of how much the system needs to change to support human development. For the most part, the current model of K–12 education is a sorting machine grounded in language, logic, and recall, not an elegant system of learning that promotes lifelong growth and unleashes human potential. I began to think about how we might change that. How do schools change? How do organizations and systems change? Is changing an existing school system even possible?

The Core of Change Is Learning

Coaching leaders gave me a vantage point to observe just how difficult it is for an organization to change—and how challenging it is for a leader to lead change effectively. Change puts us into uncharted waters. During change, we meet the edge of what we know and are able to do.

I began to dig into the question "How do organizations change?" and to research what the leading theorists have learned and if there were models out there that would help me better understand what I was witnessing. I read many books on the topic of organizational change, participated in workshops, and interviewed experts who were leading this work. I learned the difference between an adaptive challenge and a technical problem (Heifitz, Grashow, & Linsky, 2009), how to build a "dual operating system of change" (Kotter, 2014), and the importance of managing human transition through change (Bridges & Bridges, 2017). Systems thinking (Senge et al., 2000) helped me understand the human and organizational depth of the work.

As I distilled all of this knowledge from such a wide range of experts and practitioners, one big idea came to the front: The core of change is learning. An organization going through change essentially puts the entire organization into a container of learning and growth. The efficacy of that container to help the adults learn is directly proportional to the organization's ability to change. The term *learning organization* is used frequently, yet it is one of the most challenging states for any organization to reach and maintain.

All of this theory was well and good, but it was time to put it into practice. I was eager to use these tools and frameworks and to work with schools directly.

Which brings me back to the difficulty of change and the fact that organizations don't change unless the people within them change.

Change Is a Developmental Task

This book is a distillation of what I have learned about the education system and what it takes to create and lead the kind of change we want to see in our schools. I hope this book is a voice of common sense, reality, and hope for what it takes to lead change inside and outside the education system.

This book is for anyone who is designing, leading, or participating in this level of change: change that supports students in learning the skills, knowledge, and habits of mind that will enable them to thrive in an unknowable future. It is centered on the premise that, when we ask schools to change, we are asking human beings to change and this requires special tools and a human-centered approach. We cannot change the heart of the system without enabling the hearts and minds of those who give their all every single day to making schools work.

The purpose of this book is to equip education change leaders with a practical framework and human-centered tools and resources to lead meaningful, sustainable change.

I hope you use this book as a guide and resource as you lead yourself and your community on the path of change. It is not structured as a step-by-step guide, but rather as a means by which you can create your own unique path. No two schools or districts are exactly alike, therefore it is up to each community and its leaders to build and navigate the path that is unique to them.

This book is structured to help you design your own path.

Before beginning any journey, it is important to know where you are headed. In Chapter 1, I describe the new North Star of education, that is, the skills, knowledge, and habits of mind that our children need to enable them to thrive as young adults and beyond. There is a rising tide of consensus regarding these skills and knowledge, and a growing tribe of schools, districts, charter networks, and support organizations who are leading the way in this work. This chapter will invite you to think about your own answer to "What's Worth Learning?" and whether or not you see this reflected in your school's daily work—for students and adults alike.

Chapter 2 explores the question "How do we redesign an existing system?" When leading this level of change in schools, the pedagogy needs to reflect the outcomes we seek—and if we are changing pedagogy, then the culture needs to change too. You will learn the key shifts that need to take place when moving from the industrial model of education to a postindustrial model and you will be invited to think about where your school or district lies on that continuum. This chapter also defines three different kinds of change and underscores the importance of understanding the kind of change you are leading and how that will impact your decisions and your approach to leading the change.

Having gotten clear on your North Star, and the kind of change you are leading, Chapter 3 identifies five success factors that will support your change. Think of these success factors as jigsaw puzzle pieces that need to be in place in order to support the change you seek. At its core, this is developmental work. Moving from a siloed, subject-oriented curriculum to an agile, flexible system of learning that transcends subjects requires many of us to build new skills and an ongoing capacity for change and adaptation. Understanding that this work is both long term and developmental will help you navigate the change journey ahead.

Chapter 4 follows on from the success factors described in the previous chapter by introducing a number of strategies that you can implement in your school or district. Please make these suggestions your own, and amend those you find helpful as you see fit.

An integral part of leading others through change is leading yourself through change. I often remind school and district leaders that they cannot hope to lead others through change if they are not being reflective and supportive of their own learning on this path. Chapter 5, grounded in Joseph Campbell's (1973) work on the Hero's Journey, is not just for principals, superintendents, or people in formal positions of power. It is for anyone who has a vision for change that will help unleash student potential. Whether you are a teacher, administrator, parent, policymaker, entrepreneur, or interested citizen, I hope you will see yourself in the stories in this chapter and commit to leading the change you want to see.

I wrote this book for practical visionaries—people who want to know what works, to craft a meaningful vision for their community's children, and to have access to resources and tools that will help speed implementation and navigate the inevitable challenges along the way. The book is structured to help you design your own path; to that end, I encourage you to download the "Roadmap for Change" (Figure I.1) from the book's website at www .the-IFL.org/TheHumanSide to capture your insights and ideas for action. Then take your roadmap, share it with others, and most importantly, put those ideas into action.

Figure I.1 • Roadmap for Change

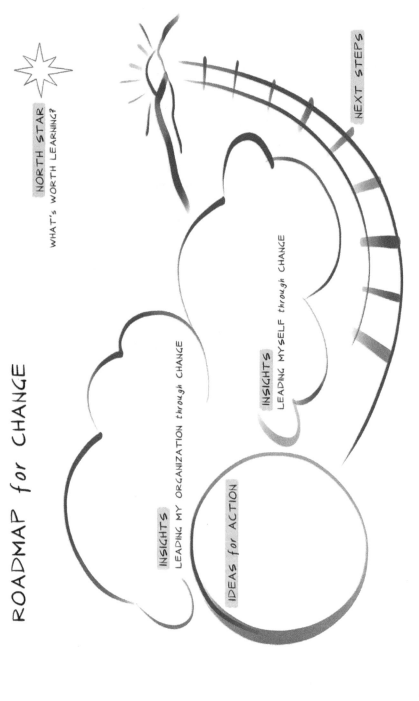

ROADMAP for CHANGE

NORTH STAR
WHAT's WORTH LEARNING?

INSIGHTS
LEADING MY ORGANIZATION through CHANGE

INSIGHTS
LEADING MYSELF through CHANGE

IDEAS for ACTION

NEXT STEPS

Source: Illustration by Kelvy Bird.

online resources ⚄ Available for download at **www.the-IFL.org/TheHumanSide**

We need hundreds of thousands of people working to change the system. There is no singular intervention that will change the system from a century-plus-old stagnant bureaucracy to a flexible, individualized system that unleashes human potential. There is no single policy, new school model, app, charismatic leader, test, or piece of research that will precipitate the level of change that we need. It will take many, many people working at all levels inside and outside the system if we are to see real and sustainable change within this decade.

If this kind of change resonates with you, I hope this book is an inspiration to keep doing your work (or to start doing it) and a guide for when things get tough—which they will.

Change is messy; it's complex and the variables are multivariate. I have had the privilege of working with leaders inside and outside the system who want to create sustainable, lasting change. What I have come to learn is that the process of change invites the adults to grow beyond their current skill set. Change is an inherently developmental task. Learning is inherently developmental. At school, we are developing human beings, not test takers. The opportunity before us is to leverage every single tool at our disposal to create the kind of learning environments that do not produce standardized young adults, but rather singular adults who know the capacity of their mind; who feel their own sense of agency; and who have the skills and courage to design, build, and live a life of their own choosing.

This work has shown me time and time again that this process of change invites the adults to learn the same skills, knowledge, and habits that we want our children to learn. Do you know the capacity of your own mind? Do you believe you can lead change that has an impact? Do you believe you can build a life of your own choosing? The majority of us were "raised" in the old system and we find ourselves with the task of being a hospice worker to the old and a midwife to the new (Leicester, 2013). This brings us to the edge of what we know and are currently able to do. It brings up our mental models, belief systems, values, and our very sense of self. If you are part of the tribe changing the education system, you will meet the edge of your current knowledge and skill set.

At the same time, there is tremendous power in coming together, in facing our fears, and in committing to the work ahead. It's scary, but it's exhilarating too. In writing this book, I have gotten really clear on what I know needs to change, my own personal North Star, and how I can help others. If what I write here resonates with you, I hope you will join me in doing the work that is in your heart to do. I share my story, and the story of others, in the hopes that you find yourself in these pages. Your experience in this work is unique; you will agree with some of the views here and disagree with others. That's good. That's healthy. At the same time, you are on a journey that has a cadence, signposts, and a path. If you engage in this work at its deepest levels, you will be transformed. And when we are transformed, the system will follow.

" We are preparing our students for success in their century, not mine. "

—PAM MORAN, SUPERINTENDENT, ALBEMARLE DISTRICT, VIRGINIA

Chapter 1

WHAT'S WORTH LEARNING? YOUR NORTH STAR

"What's Worth Learning?"

David Perkins kicked off his 2006 course, Educating for the Unknown, with this question.

The question has followed me around ever since.

My answer to the question has been distilled over the years, working with adults as a leadership trainer and coach; helping them learn the skills to build, lead, and be part of teams; navigate change; and the core of it all, to build and lead a life of their own choosing. After almost two decades of working with adults as they build the skills necessary to thrive at work and in life, I notice the same themes coming up time and time again. These used to be called "soft skills," a misnomer, as they are among the most challenging to learn and master as adults. I call them *worthy skills*: the skills that are neither easy nor soft, AND are worth learning.

Figure 1.1 describes the skills and habits of mind that we need in order to thrive as adults in our volatile, uncertain, complex and ambiguous (VUCA) world. For many of us, entering adulthood involves unlearning what we learned through a standardized system of education and learning a host of new skills essentially from scratch, skills that we could have been building much earlier as children. The World Economic Forum "The Future of Jobs" report (2016) cites the top three skills needed to thrive in 2020 as complex problem solving, critical thinking, and creativity. These same skills were identified over a decade ago by the Partnership for 21st Century Learning in Washington, DC—skills that are required for success at work—and, I would argue, in life as well.

A Rising Tide of Consensus

While there is much debate on what ails our education system, we are witnessing a rising tide of consensus regarding our collective answer to the "What's Worth Learning?" question. There is widespread agreement that the basic literacy requirements of the industrial model of education are the floor, not the ceiling, and that we need to set our sights higher for our children. Tony Wagner's book, *The Global Achievement Gap* (2014),

Figure 1.1 • What's Worth Learning?

Source: Illustration by Kelvy Bird.

describes the seven survival skills, and Sir Ken Robinson and Lou Aronica's book, *Creative Schools* (2016), describes eight core competencies. The Deeper Learning Network at the Hewlett Foundation (2013) focuses on six competencies and the Partnership for 21st Century Skills describes a framework for 21st century learning (2017) (see Figure 1.2).

As you can see from Figure 1.2, there is significant overlap and consensus. There is much more that binds us than separates us when it comes to our individual and collective answer to the question "What's Worth Learning?"

Amid this growing consensus, it is vital for schools and communities to come together and to ask themselves, "What's Worth Learning?" Our answer to this question should be the North Star that directs the work of a school or district as it embarks on its journey of change. Figure 1.2 is helpful as a jumping-off point, but it is important for communities to ask themselves this question from first principles in order to orient the process of redesigning the system accordingly.

There is an additional level to the question "What's Worth Learning?" that speaks to the process of redesigning the system and of the change

Figure 1.2 • Growing Consensus

Tony Wagner's The Global Achievement Gap	Sir Ken Robinson's Creative Schools	Hewlett Foundation's Deeper Learning Network	Partnership for 21st Century Skills	Institute for the Future of Learning Worthy Skills
Critical thinking and problem solving Collaboration across networks and leading by influence Agility and adaptability Initiative and entrepreneurship Effective oral and written communication Accessing and analyzing information Curiosity and imagination	Curiosity Creativity Criticism Communication Collaboration Compassion Composure Citizenship	Mastery of core academic content Critical thinking and complex problem solving Collaboration Effective communication Learning how to learn An "academic mindset"	Learning and innovation skills (the 4Cs): Communication Collaboration Creativity Critical thinking Life and career skills Information, media, and technology skills Key subjects—3Rs and 21st century themes	Self-directed learning Creativity and innovation Planning, adaptability, and agility Strengths awareness and application Self-efficacy Global citizenship Relationship building Critical thinking and problem solving

Sources: Adapted from Wagner (2014), Robinson & Aronica (2016), Hewlett Foundation (2013), and Partnership for 21st Century Skills (2017).

process itself, and it is one that I see rarely discussed or made explicit. **Children cannot learn these skills and habits of mind if the adults are not given the opportunity to learn them as well—and it is these very same skills and habits of mind that are necessary to lead and implement change.** Change that is human centered. Change that recognizes we are not widgets on a manufacturing line, but rather complex human beings with natural cycles of development that can be structured, nurtured, and supported—not as an afterthought to a change management plan, but as the very means by which the change will be realized.

Adults and institutions need to unlearn old habits and learn postindustrial-era skills in parallel fashion with the students. The skills in Figure 1.1, while not an exhaustive list, are skills that adults need to be able to lead and implement a more human-centered change process in our schools. These are the skills that not only help us thrive in the workplace, but thrive as human beings as well. If we agree with Einstein that "[w]e cannot solve our problems with the same thinking that created them," we need to equip our children with the skills, knowledge, and habits of mind that will enable them to address the problems that *we* created—and *we*, the adults, are playing catch-up in learning those same skills.

To help bring the skills in Figure 1.1 to life, I describe each of them below through both of these lenses, that is, student and adult: Emmy Ryder, graduate of Kent Innovation High in Grand Rapids, Michigan, describes her experience learning these skills in high school, while Lisa Abel Palmieri, Head of School and Chief Learning Officer at Holy Family Academy in Pittsburgh, Pennsylvania, describes the skills from the perspective of a school leader supporting adults and leading change.

As we explore the skills, you will notice how interrelated and interdependent the skills are, for example, questions are the genesis of creativity—the more those questions come from the learner, and the more they are directly linked to helping the learner build awareness of her strengths, the more powerful the learning experience. When solving a problem in a team, it is important to build relationships, manage conflict, and remain adaptable in the face of changing information and circumstances. So while these skills are described separately, they become even more powerful as a unified whole.

As you reflect on these skills, think about your own school or district. What is worth learning for your children? How might your answer be similar or different? How do those skills, knowledge, and habits of mind correlate to the skills, knowledge, and habits of mind that the adults will be invited to learn as part of your change process?

Worthy Skill 1: Self-Directed Learning

"In times of change learners inherit the earth; while the learned find themselves beautifully equipped to deal with a world that no longer exists."

—Eric Hoffer

What are your questions?

The power of any learning endeavor is to nurture and grow the learner's innate desire and ability to learn. We are all born curious. Each of us peppered our parents in our early years with relentless questions. Tom Barrett describes his son George's questions in hilarious and awe-inspiring fashion in his book, *Can Computers Keep Secrets? How a Six-Year-Old's Curiosity Could Change the World* (2013):

- "Why do brains work at night?"
- "What is the crumbliest thing in the world?"
- "If you had superpowers, how would you control them?"
- "Do pigs think in human, but talk in pig?"
- "What would defeat electricity?"

We live our life in the direction of our questions. Ideally our questions engage, inspire, and stretch us. We have the opportunity to follow our questions as adults—and those inspirational teachers, teachers such as Tom Barrett, invite their students to do so on a daily basis.

Questions are the starting point of creativity, and questions are at the heart of effective learning. In kindergarten we followed the trail of our questions, but as we progressed through the system, our questions became second-rate citizens to the questions in the textbook. Students and teachers who have the temerity to follow their own questions, in spite of this conditioning, too often find themselves in defiance of the system that should be supporting that seed of learning.

Emmy Ryder's story is an example of what happens when a student is invited to ask her own questions and is given ownership of her learning in a meaningful way. I first met Emmy during her junior year in high school through her writing on the New Tech Network blog where she described in clear terms *"playing the game of school"* and its deleterious impact on her intrinsic motivation to learn. In an excerpt from her blog (2013), Emmy wisely notes how, at age 14, she didn't care about learning; she cared about the grade. You can see in Emmy's writing how that shifted for her as she was given more and more ownership of her learning:

When I was in 8th grade, grades and being on top were a big deal to me. I was that kid who constantly checked the online gradebook. I always finished homework and stressed over tests. . . . Even if I understood the content, I did the worksheet anyway.

Why? For the grade.

I never really questioned the content. I just scrambled to write down all the notes. I never cared if I was going to use it in 10 years. . . . I cared about the grade.

I wanted high grades. I wanted As. I was pretty close minded. Not because I chose this path, but because this is how I had been trained since kindergarten. Grades are everything. . . . I was a narrow-minded student, with one goal, grades (not learning: grades). Basically, the steps I took were sit down, shut up, and listen, then go home and study.

[Since joining Kent Innovation High] Now I question nearly everything. Why IS the sky blue? The great thing is I don't receive science facts. I get my question answered with a question. Which leaves me room to explore myself, interpret the information myself and learn the information in a way which suits me. Projects usually focus on SWLO [schoolwide learning outcomes] more than content. This means I can take the content I do need to include and incorporate it as I feel necessary. I feel that when we create projects, I focus more on what I am taking out of the project, what others will take away, and what work I put into it. I want to create a product that I am satisfied with. Not just something that will get me a good grade.

I want to change the world with the projects I produce. Whether it's the whole world, my community or even just one person's life. I want to make that difference.

Source: Ryder (2013).

When Emmy joined Kent Innovation High, she found herself in a rich learning environment where students were not spoon-fed questions to ensure a predetermined outcome, but rather encouraged to dig into their own questions, find their own answers, and wrestle with messy problems. It is this process that enables those students to become active participants in their own learning, and, ultimately, to become self-directed learners.

For adults, how much of the learning and professional development is directed by the teachers' and administrators' learning goals? How might you begin to unleash the talent in your school? Lisa Abel Palmieri (*5 Qualities of Prepared Leaders in a Project-Based World*, 2017) describes her approach to directing her own learning. It includes everything from leveraging social media, working with mentors and trusted advisers, attending workshops and conferences—and the core of it all—the importance of knowing herself:

> Leadership is developed daily, not in a few days. Successful school leaders are learners first and foremost; they have the capacity to develop and improve their own skills, and practice demonstrating perseverance and the mindset necessary for a project-based world. As a learner, I regularly attend professional development events like the Deeper Learning Summit, SXSWedu, and many local events through Pittsburgh's amazing Remake Learning Network.

> Additionally, social media is a place where I connect with others to learn new practices, receive support, or share ideas—and it's open 24/7/365. As one of the founders of #DTK12CHAT, a weekly chat on design thinking in education, I have built a global PLN (personal learning network) that is available for support and to challenge my thinking.

Source: 5 Qualities of Prepared Leaders in a Project-Based World, http://www.gettingsmart.com/2017/03/5-qualities-prepared-leaders-project-based-world, by Lisa Abel Palmieri was originally published on Getting Smart (gettingsmart.com)

Lisa's reflections are a great example of how we have the opportunity to design our own personalized learning plan and the many low- or no-cost development opportunities that are available to us. When I spoke with Lisa directly regarding her experience of self-directed learning, she highlighted the importance of knowing oneself,

> Being aware of your personality and strengths and your opportunities for partnership is important—stay humble, ask for others' opinions and support. A huge piece of self-directed learning is to know yourself—and knowing when to ask others for help.

As a leader of change, as a teacher, as an adult working in education, what are your personal development goals? What does the next level of mastery in your field of practice look like? How are you tracking your progress and what kind of support are you surrounding yourself with?

When you reflect on the change that you are seeking in your school, how much autonomy are you building into the system for adults and children alike to direct their own learning and to follow the wisdom and wonder of their own questions? Are the adults and students following a predetermined path or do they have the opportunity to exercise choice and autonomy? Self-directed learning lies at the heart of shifting from a culture of compliance and consumption to a culture of independent thought and creativity.

Worthy Skill 2:
Creativity and Innovation

What are your dreams? What will you create?

In kindergarten, we created on a daily basis. As we moved through middle school and high school, too often "creativity" became something we did only in art class and something that was optional. Many of the post–No Child Left Behind (NCLB) reform efforts served to strip the arts and creativity across multiple content areas from many schools' curricula—all in pursuit of improving test scores. While many of these reforms were designed by people with good intentions, they served to take us further away from a core skill that we need to thrive as children and adults alike. If we lose our ability to dream, and if we lose the practice of courage in creating something and putting it out there, we lose our ability to follow our gut and take risks. This is one of the most challenging aspects of creativity as an adult: Embracing creativity is embracing failure, and as adults, we become programmed to avoid failure at all costs. We are products of a system where it is not OK to have the wrong answer, where there is little time or tolerance for trial and error, and where teachers are rarely invited to be creative in their classrooms.

> "The principal goal of education in the schools should be creating men and women who are capable of doing new things, not simply repeating what other generations have done; men and women who are creative, inventive, and discoverers."
>
> —Jean Piaget

Providing adults with the opportunity and support to fail and to learn in a safe environment is one of the biggest challenges of school change. I remember a teacher in a summer institute where we were discussing the change her school was leading in the next academic year. She described in detail how she wanted to partner with another teacher and create a new curriculum that would take their students out of the classroom to work on an interdisciplinary service project in the local community. She was both excited and afraid. She said that she really wanted to do the project but was unsure if the timing was right and if she could really swing it. I knew there was something else going on, something else below the surface of "enough time." I asked her, "What else?" a few times—and then we landed on the core challenge. With a shaky voice, she said, "It might go belly up. It might fail. It might be a disaster." The comment sparked the most helpful conversation of the day; her fellow teachers empathized and began discussing how the price of creativity is the openness to fail and how they might support each other through this change. Teaching is a high stakes activity, one where failures are too often seen as disasters. We need to support teachers in experimentation, reflection, and iteration of their practice. We need to support their learning.

Openly talking about the risks and opportunities of failure serves not only the adults, but is a springboard for teachers to have the same conversations with their students. Students are much more likely to create in a low stakes, safe environment where the only real failure is either not trying in the first place, or not learning from the failed attempt.

Emmy describes how creativity came from the freedom she was given to choose projects and she shares the example of a project from her eleventh-grade economics class:

> A lot of creativity came from the freedom we were given and the ability to choose what to work on. I remember a project I loved in 11th grade for economics class. We were focusing on both preserving the environment and designing a product to market. I decided to design a self-watering flower bottle. I designed and created a prototype of the product and presented it to a panel of local business people and artists. While the objectives of the project were aligned with the schoolwide learning outcomes, we had complete freedom of choice with regard to what we choose to design, build, and present. With twenty different students, we had twenty different products.

Lisa is an expert in design thinking and has led many workshops over the years, teaching adults how to use this methodology to tap into their creativity. She believes that in order to be truly creative, to help each other and to help the students, the process has to be human centered. Can you put yourself into the shoes of the person for whom you are designing? To what extent do you understand the world of the students whose learning environment you want to improve? Lisa taps into one of the not-often discussed challenges of the system:

> It has to be about what others need, not what you think they need.

Lisa goes on to describe how we might model creativity as the adults and carve out more space for teachers to have the opportunity to create:

> [At our school] creativity and innovation are part of our values, creativity is built into how we do the everyday work—that means teachers are collaborating extensively across subject areas, and they have forty plus days of professional development per year. We try out different things, we use improv activities to warm up; everything we do in classrooms, we model in teacher professional development. It needs to be as innovative and creative for the adults as it is for the students.

How are students and adults alike in your school or district being encouraged to be creative and innovative? Is it incentivized and encouraged?

Along the continuum of "It never happens" to "It's baked into our values and how we work and learn," where would you place your school or district?

Worthy Skill 3: Planning, Adaptability, and Agility

How can you become an adaptable, agile planner?

A core skill as an adult is to be able to plan and adapt. Knowing when and how to adapt is as much an art as it is a science. One of my favorite courses to teach was Project Management 101. It was great fun helping class participants scope their projects, establish milestones, and plan their work. Invariably, one of the participants would mention the fact that plans often do not, that is never, go as planned. The class would shift into a generative discussion on the importance of planning—and the importance of adapting or throwing out the plan entirely when circumstances morph and change.

> "Plans are of little use, but planning is essential."
>
> —Winston Churchill

I would love to see courses such as Project Management 101 become obsolete for adults as a direct result of kids learning these skills at school via meaningful, real-world projects. I saw a glimpse into that future when I visited Columbus Signature Academy in Columbus, Indiana. The fourteen-year-old students described how they worked on scoping, planning, and implementing team-based projects. One of the students explained how students coach and give each other feedback on overall progress and how they adapt when things do not go according to plan. The process and protocols that they had designed and were using would rival those of any high-performing adult team.

We bump up against the need to plan and adapt when implementing change as adults. We need a plan for the change, but in equal measure, we need to hold the plan lightly. This is why getting clear on vision and purpose is so important—there are many paths that can take us there, but if we are not clear on where we are headed, chaos can and will ensue.

Emmy describes her experience of being too ambitious in one of her first projects at Kent Innovation High and how she learned how to plan, be flexible, and adapt as needed:

During one of my first video projects, I had a very specific story line that I wanted us to follow. I kept thinking that I could cram it in, but I ran out of time and the end result wasn't great. I knew it wasn't my best work. The next time I had learned my lesson. During the planning process I realized I needed to cut the story down and get clear on what the end product would look like. I remember thinking, "Instead of cramming all of this content in, let's prioritize." It taught me that it's OK to change the plan and that I need to be flexible.

Lisa shares an interesting take on this skill for adults. She talks about being a "navigator" as a leader of change:

> Being a navigator means I know the policies and what could be a roadblock. How do I make a crazy idea happen? What can prevent it? I make sure I have a response for it. I want to be sure I have an answer for things that can be roadblocks, before they are asked. It's important to anticipate the barriers.

Being adaptable is a key part of leading any successful change effort. You are almost 100 percent guaranteed that your plan will not work out as planned. BUT you need a plan. Hold it lightly and stay on course, or in Lisa's words, "Keep the quest and find ways around roadblocks."

How might you redesign learning in your school or district in such a way that students are given the opportunity to plan, learn, and adapt? How are you building that skill set for yourself as you lead a change and how might your colleagues be partners in planning, adapting, and reorienting during the change process?

Worthy Skill 4: Strengths Awareness and Application

"Everybody is a genius. But if you judge a fish by its ability to climb a tree, it will spend its whole life believing that it is stupid."

—Anonymous, although often credited to Albert Einstein

There are some things you can do better than most. Do you know what they are?

Building on your personal strengths has been proven to lead to success, but I see too many adults asking themselves this question, in many cases for the first time, in their mid- to late adulthood.

Our educational system, for the most part, values strengths in logic, language, and recall, and it diminishes, or ignores, strengths that do not fall within those narrow domains. How might we begin to understand these individual talents better—for children and adults alike?

Before she went to Kent Innovation High, Emmy thought her strengths were in memorizing information and doing what was on the paper. In Emmy's words, "I learned to play the game of school." As she progressed in her studies at Kent Innovation High, she learned that her strengths were public speaking, organizing and giving tours, and helping others—strengths that had lain dormant during her previous high school experience.

> With time and a different kind of learning environment, my strengths flourished. How was the environment different? For the first time, I was surrounded by people who supported and pushed me to do my best, I was working with real organizations, and I could see where they needed help. It felt good to be able to help other people in those organizations. A good example was the book project we did when we

worked with a local children's hospital. We designed, wrote, and produced books for kids and we related them back to the nuclear topics we were studying in physics. I discovered when I am doing my best to help other people, that's when my strengths really kick in.

As a school leader, Lisa describes how she works from a strengths perspective, not a deficits perspective, when managing and leading the adults in her school:

Every new hire that comes into our school takes the Gallup (n.d.) StrengthsFinder survey as part of our onboarding process. It is the foundation for our mentorship program for new staff. Every class in the school is co-taught; we partner master teachers with teachers who have one to two years' experience. We discuss their respective strengths—how they align, how they are different, how you can grow them, and how to build on each other's strengths.

I also use strengths to talk about team development and to help me receive the feedback I need. I have the "Activator" strength and have a strong drive to start new things; sometimes I overuse that strength and need to tone it down. I rely on my team to give me that feedback when I need it and it helps us to create a positive culture of development for everyone.

In our postindustrial world, understanding our talents and strengths has shifted from a "nice to have" to a "must have." How might we establish learning environments that enable students and adults to dive into their strengths and their talents in a deep and meaningful way?

Worthy Skill 5: Self-Efficacy

Do you believe you can?

In many ways, the current education system perpetuates learned helplessness. The underlying message of "college for all," while well intentioned, tells students that you need a college degree to be successful. You have two choices: Go to college and have a chance of success, or don't go to college and be relegated to a life of minimum wage. I remember talking with a group of students in Maine where one of the students asked if she *had* to go to college. I asked her to expand on the question and she said, "When do I get to do what I want to do? Do I have to go to college and then do what I want to do afterward, or can I start doing what I want to do now?"

It struck me that I have the same conversation with adults all the time in their work. Conversations where adults tell me that first they need a master's degree before they can start doing the work they want to do; For example, my friend Melissa, a schoolteacher, thought she needed an MBA before she started her business. In addition to teaching for almost a decade, Melissa had worked for the same amount of time in her family's small

"If I have the belief that I can do it, I shall surely acquire the capacity to do it even if I may not have it at the beginning."

—Mahatma Gandhi

business. She had a host of skills already that would serve her in building her business. No MBA required. "Learned helplessness" and "waiting for permission" get in the way of our dreams, and the education system, in many ways, perpetuates both.

I am not saying that undergraduate and postgraduate degrees are unnecessary; there are many fields that require these credentials. What I am saying is that the unintended consequence of "college for all" negates a noncollege choice and in many cases perpetuates "learned helplessness."

Shawn Humphrey calls himself the Blue Collar Professor; he is on a mission to help young people tap into their agency and self-efficacy. This is not just something that we add on as a forty-five-minute block on a Tuesday. It is the blood that runs through the veins of an enlightened approach to learning. Shawn calls it "Tribal Teaching":

> We are on a journey to activate your agency. It will be perilous. Struggle will be ever present. Your demons will be your constant companion. They will sabotage your efforts. They will create setbacks. They will induce long durations of self-doubt. They will make the prospect of failure grow and grow. But, you will carry on. You will fight. You will battle. You will scratch and claw and punch. You will slay. And in that moment of victory, you will have reclaimed your humanity. You will have tasted freedom. It will taste good. You will want more.

Imagine if our entire education system prepared its young adults for that level of agency.

Emmy recalls a transition during her earlier years at Kent Innovation High when she learned an important lesson regarding agency and her intrinsic motivation as a learner:

> I was in 10th grade and we were working on a water project. I wasn't 100% sure of my role and I wasn't very motivated. I started to take a back seat, stopped asking questions, and continued to struggle. It did not get better as time went on. I fell more and more behind. I learned that lesson and stepped up in 11th and 12th grade. I realized that I needed to find my intrinsic motivation in the work—it was a combination of realizing what needed to be done and wanting to do it. As I developed that skill, it led to greater self-awareness and helped me push myself to complete tasks that were needed.

When supporting and nurturing the agency of adults, Lisa has some wise and very doable advice:

> [T]o support your teachers, to help them believe in themselves and their talents, you need to get to know them. Talk to them. Make the effort to speak with everyone, particularly the quiet ones. Know your staff. In a large school district that can be hard, but building-level

principals can. You need to go into a teacher's classroom for more than one or two observations per year. Eat lunch with people, go to the out-of-school activities, and hit the Happy Hour. Oftentimes out of school, people feel more free to say what they mean. Help a teacher who might lack confidence. Know your teachers, know their talents, and tailor opportunities to help them grow.

As a leader, you have the opportunity to establish an environment that either increases or decreases the sense of self-efficacy in your students and in your staff. How much agency and choice do your students have in a typical day of school? Are they given autonomy and support to work on projects that align not only with the standards, but with their interests as well? What about the adults? Do they have active voice and responsibility in the running of the school? How might you redesign your school's systems and processes to provide adults and students with more agency and choice?

Worthy Skill 6: Global Citizenship

Are you ready for a global and interdependent world?

We are more connected than ever via technology. In equal measure, we experience extreme division and separateness. I grew up during the Troubles of Northern Ireland against the backdrop of people declaring hate for each other in the name of religion. I believe every single person on this planet has more in common with each other than we realize.

If I had a magic wand, I would ask that every young person take an ancestry DNA test and learn the complexity of their ancestral composition. Tolerance, empathy, and connection with others "different" than ourselves is not a "nice to have"—it's a nonnegotiable that our young people don't repeat the same mistakes that we have made in the name of religion and of perceived sovereignty.

The United Nations Educational, Scientific and Cultural Organization (UNESCO; 2015) notes, "Global citizenship refers to a sense of belonging to a broader community and common humanity. It emphasises political, economic, social and cultural interdependency and interconnectedness between the local, the national and the global."

This can happen today in all our schools, if we choose, and organizations such as UNESCO, in partnership with the Asia Society (n.d., asiasociety .org/education), provide a depth of resources to help make it a reality.

During her time at Kent Innovation High in Michigan, Emmy got to know students who were leading exciting projects all over the world via the regular Twitter chats she hosted:

Living in the 21st century with its technological advances lends itself to different connections and pushes your learning. You don't have to

> "If I knew something that would serve my country but would harm mankind, I would never reveal it; for I am a citizen of humanity first and by necessity, and a citizen of France second, and only by accident."
>
> —Charles de Montesquieu

work with the same people all the time; you can branch out and find people you need. Through Twitter I have sent ideas back and forward internationally. I feel great that I have those connections, and that I can reach out and build more global relationships throughout career and life.

Lisa has the vantage point of having worked in diverse learning environments including an all girls' boarding school, the U.S. Navy, One Schoolhouse, and her current school, Holy Family Academy. Lisa turns the notion of global citizenship being "out there" beyond the school walls on its head. Inside many schools resides a rich tapestry of races, religions, and backgrounds. This is a tremendous opportunity for learning, and yet, too often, these children are asked to leave their culture at the door of the school.

Especially important for educational leaders that do not look like their students is to unpack their privilege and uncover societal, institutional, and personal bias that they bring into their schools/districts. According to Professor Christopher Emdin, urban youth especially are often expected to leave their day-to-day life and experiences behind and assimilate into the culture of schools. This process is a form of self-repression that is traumatic and directly impacts what happens in our classrooms.

Leaders with a focus on equity create safe and trusting environments and provide resources that are respectful of a student's culture, not working to change it. This might be more important than ever right now to prepare all students in our global society for a project-based world. If we don't, the socioeconomic and racial gaps of the creative class will grow even wider. Educational leaders must create a culture where ways of seeing and engaging will challenge the status quo by naming uncomfortable realities and unequal conditions.

Lisa helped me understand that "global citizenship" does not just mean building relationships with our fellow citizens in other countries; it can be something as simple and complex as embracing the global citizenry already existing in our schools. This includes hiring teachers and administrators that reflect the student body and honoring and nurturing the multivariate traditions, cultures, and languages represented.

Lisa admits that it is challenging work. She has had success in hiring administrators to reflect her student body but has more challenges hiring teachers from her local area. Undaunted, she is now reaching out to colleges and universities outside her city—offering new recruits two years of free housing on campus and the opportunity to be mentored by her master teachers. It will take time, but the ultimate goal is that the adults in the building reflect the diversity of the students in the building.

What are your opportunities to expand what is possible from a Global Citizenship perspective in your school or district?

Worthy Skill 7: Relationship Building

Can you have a skillful difficult conversation?

This is one of the most challenging things to do as an adult. Can you assert your own needs in a relationship (be it work or personal) and listen, truly listen, while the other person asserts theirs? Difficult conversations, managing conflict, toxic teams—these are amongst the thorniest problems at work and they follow us home as well.

The social dynamics in any school provide the opportunity to learn these skills from an early age, and we have choices with regard to how we do this, not as a stand-alone class, but as a value and artifact of the school's culture. I recall a principal with whom I was working who told me that bullying in the first month of the academic year at his middle school had become standard operating procedure with a line at his door of students waiting to be reprimanded. We were working that summer with newly formed teacher teams on setting a vision for the school and planning what the first week of school might look like. The teachers decided to spend the first week establishing a welcoming, inclusive learning environment that focused on student engagement and students exploring their hopes and dreams for the year ahead. The students described their expectations of themselves, their fellow classmates, and the teacher. They brainstormed goals for the year and talked about "our classroom" and how every person had a part to play in it being a fun and challenging learning environment. A month into the new school year, the principal noted there were zero incidents of bullying during that first month. While correlation does not necessarily equal causation, I do believe the students' work in establishing those safe learning environments lessened the bullying.

> "Truth is everybody is going to hurt you: you just gotta find the ones worth suffering for."
>
> —Bob Marley

The adults in that same school faced similar challenges building relationships. For the first time that year, they were collaborating as a team, planning lessons together, visiting each other's classrooms, and giving each other feedback. It was tough. The adults struggled as they went through the forming, storming, and norming stages of team development (Tuckman, 1965). They struggled adhering to the meeting norms they had established and agreed upon. They struggled to have direct difficult conversations with themselves and with each other. In many ways, adults can have just as much difficulty building effective working relationships as the students do.

From the student perspective, Emmy notes how project-based learning helped her learn how to create deep relationships—be they professional or personal—and how to manage conflict:

[Project-based learning] forces you to work with others and put yourself out there and to be vulnerable. I built relationships inside my school and outside my school through my projects. I would often contact a number of folks at Michigan Education Tech. They would give me feedback on my papers, ask me questions, and provide advice. Sometimes my peer review in class might have been short and I would email them ask them to look over my work with me.

Working on projects also helps you to manage conflict—every team has its struggles and I learned how to get through them. There was a time when one member on our team wasn't fulfilling their responsibilities. It was a hard conversation to have. It was my friend and I didn't want to cross the line and damage the relationship. It's like at work: you need to have the hard conversation and try to separate the two. The conversation went OK, it could have gone better, it was taken a bit like an attack, but after the initial conversation, we talked it through. The follow-up conversation really helped.

Emmy was building skills in her teenage years that, truthfully, took me into my midtwenties and beyond to learn. Managing conflict is part of life. It is important that we build these skills much earlier, and schools such as Kent Innovation High provide the environment for students to learn these skills as a natural part of a well-designed project-based curriculum.

From the adult perspective, Lisa shares the importance of building relationships in achieving the school mission and building a culture of deep learning:

Diversity of people, ideas, and action makes innovation happen in schools and the workplace. At Holy Family Academy, all of the classes are interdisciplinary and co-taught by teams of teachers. With particular focus on the personality and experience of our faculty, teaching teams are purposely diverse.

She goes on to highlight the importance of building relationships with families and the broader community to support students, and shares the example of "Jason":

Jason was as bright as can be—he was a really engaged student and was excelling. He was in an amazing engineering program and really thriving. Then he failed three classes. How was he failing when we knew he was so cognitively bright? After many conversations, we learned that he had extreme anxiety because his mother is undocumented and he was worried that she would be deported. He was paying the family bills by working 30 hours a week, some nights until midnight. If you just call Mom in that kind of scenario and try to fix the situation in one phone call, you are not going to make much headway. It took a home visit, a dinner, and four meetings until we reached the point where we could talk about resources and how to set Jason up for success. You have to take the time to build relationships.

Schools are inherently about relationships. If you are shifting away from the factory model of education, that means you are embracing teacher teams and interdisciplinary collaborative work. It means working with students and their families in partnership. How might you help students collaborate with one another? How might you help the adults collaborate with one another? How might you partner, in a meaningful way, with student families?

Worthy Skill 8: Critical Thinking and Problem Solving

How do you answer a non-Googleable question?

My friend the engineer is always on the hunt to find people who can solve problems. He has been doing this work for twenty years and has noted a trend in the last seven: that it is becoming harder to find people who can think independently and solve problems. He has a few theories as to why: standardized curriculum, rote learning, "safest path to college" check boxes, no start-up experience. Is this reality or the rantings of a curmudgeon? I don't know, but I do know that school, for the most part, does not support its teachers in giving students thorny challenges that they may or may not be able solve, and that students too often know there is a "right" answer and it's at the back of the textbook.

> "All his life, Klaus had believed that if you read enough books, you could solve any problem, but now he wasn't so sure."
>
> —Lemony Snicket, *The Bad Beginning*

Eric Mazur, physics professor, completely changed how he designed and structured his curriculum when he realized that, while his incoming students knew the equations and laws in physics, many were unable to use them to solve real-world problems: "When asked, for instance, to compare the forces in a collision between a heavy truck and a light car, many students firmly believe the heavy truck exerts a larger force" (2007). I'll admit that I did too—despite learning the equations in high school.

Critical thinking and creative problem solving are as much about how a teacher facilitates a class as they are about the specifics of curriculum. Emmy describes how, when she would ask for an answer to a question in class, the teacher would ask her a question in return. Invariably that question would provide guidance on how Emmy could find the answer out for herself. Emmy notes that this skill can be learned in any classroom:

It can be done anywhere if you have the mindset. My advice would be to make small changes and push for change yourself. You can make small changes in a classroom, or any setting, just by asking different questions, throwing our different ideas, forcing people to take a different look at things and to think things through for themselves.

Lisa describes critical thinking as "the idea of applying knowledge with a bias for action" and she notes that it takes time to build the confidence to apply your learning—with students and adults alike. She notes how oftentimes her newer teachers are not confident in their skills; she uses the design thinking framework to help teachers prototype lessons, think critically about what worked well and what might be improved next time, and encourages them to try it again. She underscores that critical thinking takes perseverance—perseverance to try something new, to look at it from multiple angles, and to keep iterating as you go.

Critical thinking and problem solving link strongly to self-efficacy. Evolving from an industrial-era model of education requires a culture shift from the patriarchal model of management to one of self-efficacy and partnership. Do your students feel empowered to identify and solve their own problems or is there a culture of waiting for the teacher to both define and solve the problem? Similarly, how does this show up with the adults in your school? Do the teachers and administrators feel empowered to define and solve their own problems or is there a culture of waiting for leadership to both define and solve the problem? How might you begin to make the shift via the process of change?

In this chapter, we explored the multidimensional nature of the work when we answer the question "What's Worth Learning?" It impacts not only what we value in a child's development, but also that of the adult's and his or her changing role as the change process unfolds. Let's go a level deeper in the next chapter as we follow the "What's Worth Learning?" question with "How Is It Best Learned?" (Perkins, 2006)

Key Points

- There is widespread agreement that the basic literacy requirements of the industrial model of education are the floor, not the ceiling, of school performance and that we need to set our sights higher for our children.

- We need to redefine what's worth learning for the 21st century.

- There is a rising tide of consensus as to the skills, knowledge, and habits of mind that will help us thrive as adults in the 21st century. These skills are interrelated and interdependent.

- Amid this growing consensus, it is vital for schools and communities to come together and to ask themselves, "What's Worth Learning?" Your community's answer to this question is the North Star that directs the work on its journey of change.

- Worthy Skills are

  1. Self-Directed Learning
  2. Creativity and Innovation
  3. Planning, Adaptability, and Agility
  4. Strengths Awareness and Application

5. Self-Efficacy

6. Global Citizenship

7. Relationship Building

8. Critical Thinking and Problem Solving

- Children cannot learn these skills and habits of mind, if the adults are not given the opportunity to learn them as well—and it is these very same skills and habits of mind that are necessary to lead and implement change.

Questions for Reflection and Action

- What do you think our children should know and be able to do by the time they graduate high school? What are the worthy skills?

- If you have already defined "What's Worth Learning?" in your mission or vision statement, are these skills and knowledge reflected in the day-to-day experience of teachers and students?

- If not, how might you incorporate the desired skills and knowledge into your school's curricula and pedagogy?

- How might you incorporate the desired skills and knowledge into your school's talent development process for adults? How might the development of those skills support the change process?

- What additional questions did this chapter prompt for you?

- What action items did this chapter prompt for you?

CHAPTER 1 | What's Worth Learning? Your North Star   27

" If we taught babies to talk as most skills are taught in school, they would memorize lists of sounds in a predetermined order and practice them alone in a closet. **"**

—LINDA DARLING-HAMMOND, *BE THE CHANGE: REINVENTING SCHOOL FOR STUDENT SUCCESS*

Chapter 2

HOW DO WE REDESIGN AN EXISTING SYSTEM?

The Pedagogy Needs to Reflect the Outcomes We Seek

When we decide that skills such as creativity, collaboration, and critical thinking are important for our students to learn, we quickly bump into the question "How are these skills best learned?" (Perkins, 2006).

The questions of "What's Worth Learning?" and "How Is It Best Learned?" (Perkins, 2006) are inextricably linked. A teacher cannot be expected to teach risk taking if students and teachers alike are not allowed to experiment and fail in the learning process. Collaboration requires group work, self-assessment, peer assessment, and iterative reflection and changes in behavior—and teachers being given the space and time to work as teams. Creative problem solving requires a student to think for herself, not what the back of the textbook says she should think—and for teachers to have the autonomy to do the same.

The industrial age model of education is grounded in a behaviorist theory of "child as empty vessel waiting to be filled" and that learning is a matter of disseminating content—content that is dutifully consumed, retained, and regurgitated for a test.

I am not saying that rote memorization should never be used. However, the pendulum has swung much too far in the aftermath of No Child Left Behind with its heavy focus on worksheets and rote memorization. It is one tool available in a much broader toolkit.

What was your most impactful learning experience? Why was it so impactful? A well-designed learning experience stretches a learner out of his comfort zone and supports and develops his intrinsic motivation to learn. Teachers know this, yet the system is designed in such a way as to work actively against sound pedagogical practices and what it takes to learn the skills described earlier.

So how are these skills best learned? **By going back to the roots of how we have learned for thousands of years—through hands-on interdisciplinary**

real-world work, failure and trying again, exposure to mentors and guides, through story, through repeated practice with reflection and feedback, and by having the freedom to take risks.

By way of example, here are a few questions to help prompt how a number of the Worthy Skills might be learned; this is not an exhaustive list, but an illustration of how the pedagogy must reflect and support the outcomes you have determined as part of your school or district's North Star.

> **Self-Directed Learning**—If we want learners to be more self-directed, we need to give them the opportunity to direct their own learning. That is not to say that state-level standards are to be rejected, but rather to recognize there is incredible capacity for a learner to choose his or her path in learning in meeting those standards—and that that choice is most effectively embedded in a learner's own interests. What intrigues your students? What are their questions? What is most present in their lives right now and how can that be used as a vehicle to direct their learning? What about the adults? What are their short-, medium-, and long-term career goals? What are their passions and interests? What are the skills, knowledge, and habits of mind they hope to build in support of the school's North Star?

> **Creativity and Innovation**—Change is often viewed as a process that must be managed and controlled. What if we flipped that notion and embraced change as an ongoing, iterative process that provides the opportunity for students and adults alike to actively create learning that is meaningful? On any given day or week in your school, how much opportunity do the students and the adults have to create and innovate? How much "new learning" would you like to create in your school this year? When you reflect on the changes you would like to lead in your school or district, how might you unleash and support the creativity of the adults in pursuit of that change?

> **Strengths Awareness and Application**—Reflect on the students in your school. How might you help each student understand and build on their strengths as a natural and ongoing part of the learning process? How might you help adults identify, build, and apply their strengths during change?

These are just a few examples of how the Worthy Skills might be learned. When a school or district goes through the process of identifying "What's Worth Learning?" the skills, knowledge, and habits of mind identified have tremendous impact on the pedagogical practices of the teachers who are charged with the design and facilitation of that learning—and those practices are directly impacted by culture. A learner-centered, interdisciplinary, creative approach to pedagogy cannot thrive in the compliance-, control-, and consumption-oriented culture of the traditional industrial-era school.

Changing Pedagogy
Changes Your Culture

Over the years, I have visited many schools where great work is happening—schools where students are learning the skills and habits of mind that will enable them to thrive, and learning them in an integrated, holistic way. One of my most impactful experiences was visiting my first New Tech Network school, the Columbus Signature Academy, in Columbus, Indiana.

My school tour started when I was greeted at the door by two students (I was expecting adults). They welcomed me warmly, led me into a conference room, and started the conversation by asking, "What do you already know about our school and what do you want to know?" It took me aback. I wasn't prepared and I hadn't thought through my own questions. It made me realize how accustomed I had become to arriving at a school and expecting the school to dictate the important questions—without asking them of myself. Much has been written about New Tech Network's pedagogy, its interdisciplinary project-based curriculum, the role of teacher, and the focus on such skills as collaboration and creative problem solving, but my biggest takeaway from that school was that none of it works in absence of the school's culture—and that pedagogy is a mirror of school culture.

The network has three core values: trust, respect, and responsibility; these values permeate the school and provide the fertile soil for the pedagogy. Take "trust." Shortly after arriving at Columbus Signature Academy and meeting with the students in a conference room, we got up to leave the room to visit a number of classrooms. I picked up my purse (the usual fifteen-pound behemoth bag with laptop, paperwork, and books), when one of the students told me I could leave it in the room and did not need to carry it with me. For the second time in thirty minutes, I was taken aback. That bag held my wallet, keys, personal information, a recently purchased laptop, and my phone. Was it crazy for me to leave it here, in an open space, where anyone could just take it? I was embarrassed. I realized that while I stand wholeheartedly behind trusting students, there I was face-to-face with my own beliefs and lack of trust. The lack of trust that I could leave my bag in this semipublic space with students humbled me. I left the bag.

When I asked about the value of responsibility, one of the students explained to me how the school principal often repeats the phrase "We can't expect kids to be responsible if we don't give them responsibility." Then she went on to describe a number of examples, including how it is the students' responsibility to orient new students, not just the teachers'. With regard to respect, I didn't need an explanation; it was palpable. The student leaders who took me on the tour were respectful of me, themselves, their teachers, fellow students, and the school.

Over the course of that tour, Columbus Signature Academy showed me what it means for a school to truly live its values. That's when I realized that answering the question "How Is It Best Learned?" gets to heart of a school's values and culture. It's like an iceberg. Above the waterline are the elements of a great learning environment and underneath the waterline is the culture that is needed to support that learning.

If we want to change an existing traditional, industrial-era school to a flexible learning environment that prepares our children for an unknowable future, we are talking about deep culture change. Under the waterline of culture lie our mental models, beliefs, and assumptions about what's worth learning and how it is best learned. And it is that which lies under the water line that helps us understand the complexity of what it takes to truly change a system.

Let's explore the fundamental shifts required when moving from the industrial model of education to a postindustrial model and the importance of understanding the kind of change you are leading.

Moving From the Industrial Educational Model to a Postindustrial Model

On paper, everything looked solid. The school—a suburban New England school—was achieving the academic benchmarks prescribed by the state. By traditional measures, this was clearly a strong and academically successful school. This is the type of school that is often regarded as steady and solid. In this traditional context, change was not considered a necessity.

Sandra Trach became the principal in 2002 and saw something different within that same school. When she walked the hallways of the school, talked with students and teachers, and participated in classrooms, she had a sense of the untapped potential of every individual in that building. With her background in curriculum and instruction, brain-based pedagogy, and special education, Sandra had a vision to transform and elevate an already strong educational experience for the students by inspiring a new and undiscovered culture for her school community.

In Virginia, Jared Cotton experienced something similar when he became superintendent of Henry County district. The district had close to 70 percent free and reduced lunch and was meeting the passing requirements for the Virginia state tests. Why change? Wasn't this a "good" school district?

Jared had spent the six and a half years prior serving as the district lead for assessment and strategic plan work at Virginia Beach City Public Schools (VBCPS). He had witnessed firsthand how a district that excels academically in traditional measures is not necessarily preparing its students for college, career, and citizenship. Despite the fact that VBCPS students were doing well academically, according to the state standards, when the administration team participated in "learning walks" and visited classrooms, even the advanced classrooms, they did not see examples of deep thinking in action. The majority of the learning was focused on content and recall, with very few examples of critical thinking, problem solving, and students thinking for themselves. Armed with what he had learned regarding how to lead deep change at VBCPS, Jared saw a different vision for the students and the broader community in Henry County and was eager to get to work.

How do you introduce, lead, and implement change in these kinds of environments? What might a "Roadmap for Change" look like?

When I first embarked on this work, I was in search of an airtight model for change—a model I could bring to any community and say, "Here is the model that will help your district or school get from here to there—here are the guaranteed outcomes of using this model." I researched; I read; I constructed logic model after logic model—convinced the answer was out there. The irony of what I was doing dawned on me gradually. By searching for THE model, I was still keeping myself bound by industrial-model thinking. I discovered there is no single model out there that is THE model for school change. There is no model you can take off the shelf and implement with 100 percent fidelity. It is back to us being messy human beings and the fact that schools are not all the same in terms of both starting and end points in the change process.

Changing a system is one of the most challenging things to do. If we are saying that we want to support more creativity, collaboration, and appetite for risk in schools, then the organizational structure, systems, and processes must change, and change significantly, in order to support and reflect that pedagogy.

And those changes fly in the face of how a school is typically structured. The majority of school and district structures take the form of the industrial-era hierarchy, where decision making is consolidated at the top of the organization, with reduced autonomy regarding outcomes as we get closer to the classroom. If we want students to be collaborative, creative, and self-directed learners, the system in which this work happens must reflect a collaborative, creative, autonomous culture. Learning is an inherently risk-oriented enterprise. We learn most deeply when given the opportunity to try, fail, learn, and try again.

I believe an appetite for failure and "not knowing" is the heart of systems' change and helps to explain why so many school and district change initiatives fail. The system does not tolerate failure. It does not tolerate learning and, for the most part, it does not give autonomy and the role of change leadership to the people doing the actual work, that is, teachers. It is also very unforgiving to leaders who have a vision for change and who undertake the hard work of its implementation.

Having coached leaders leading this level of change, I have noticed several shifts that need to take place when moving from the industrial model of education to a postindustrial model. These shifts are not check-the-box

Figure 2.1 • **Shifting to a Postindustrial Education Model**

Industrial Schools	Postindustrial Schools
Students as passive recipients of content, exercising limited choice	Students as self-directed, entrepreneurial learners
Teacher as deliverer of content	Teacher as designer and facilitator of immersive learning environments
Little differentiation for student's individual strengths and interests	Strengths- and interest-based learning for every student
Time-based learning	Competency-based learning
Single discipline-based learning as curriculum driver	Interdisciplinary learning as curriculum driver
Learning grounded in static content and rote memorization of facts	Learning grounded in the real-world and practical application
Learning takes place on the school campus only	Learning takes place on campus and off campus, meaningful community and global partnerships
Content-based assessment via written tests or exams. Learning assessed by the teacher only	Mastery-based assessment of skills, knowledge, and habits of mind. Assessment by self, peers, teachers, and external experts

items to be completed, but rather elements that speak to the depth of the culture change that is required and to the scope of the work ahead. Figure 2.1 highlights these elements.

In reality, many of our nation's schools and districts are not solidly on one side or another—they are somewhere in between, with a growing number making the move toward the right. Think of Figure 2.1 as a continuum: Where is your school or district today and where would you like it to be in the future? Grab a pen and mark where your school currently falls in a given category with a check mark and then mark where you would like your school to be in the future with an asterisk. When you reflect on your school's North Star, and the skills, knowledge, and habits of mind with which you would like your students to graduate, which of the above shifts are required in order to support that learning? Are there elements you would add or change in this continuum?

These elements are not stand-alone and they are not the kind of changes that can be mandated. They are interrelated, interdependent, and require deep culture change. For example, making the transition from traditional tests to mastery-based assessment of skills requires that all teachers are given the autonomy, support, and professional development required to assess student mastery across multiple content areas, multiple audiences, multiple demonstrations of student performance—AND to have a shared understanding and practice amongst peers of what different levels of mastery look like. When a school commits to assessing skills and habits of mind, in addition to content, they have embarked on a journey of change that requires the people who will implement the change to be the architects and designers of that change.

In the opening paragraphs of this chapter, I mentioned Jared Cotton. Jared became the superintendent of Henry County School District in 2012. He had been hired by the school board to lead the implementation of its strategic plan. When Jared arrived at Henry County, the strategic plan had already been defined. When he looked at the vision and mission, he could see that critical thinking and creativity were already included. What was missing was a clear sense of "How will we know when we have reached our goals on the strategic plan? How will we measure success?"

This is a very common challenge with strategic plans and school change. If you were to take the vision and mission statements for ten schools, you would see a lot of very similar language—words and phrases such as *lifelong learners*, *citizenship*, *critical thinking*, and *college and career readiness*. This language may or may not bear any relation to the school's curriculum, pedagogy, and assessment practices. Jared recognized this and began the hard work of bringing groups of people together to discuss and define how they would tell if they had been successful or not in reaching their goals. Defining success in the school's terms gets to the belly of the beast. You have to redefine success for your school or district even though the state might define it by test scores—you have to change the conversation. Jared brought together leaders from his local community. He asked for their help in changing the conversation and in supporting different success measures in addition to those test scores. They agreed and supported Jared as he began the work of changing the system to align with the vision and mission in the strategic plan.

Five years after starting this work, Henry County has invested heavily in the development of its curriculum and its teachers. The district has redefined its assessment measures and is assessing what they value as stated in the district's vision and mission. Jared has aligned the instructional practices, budget, his board updates, meetings with principals, district reports, and day-to-day decisions with the district vision. After three years, Jared started to see results; after five, he started to see sustainable change begin to take hold.

Realistically, this level of change can take anywhere from five to seven years, depending on your school or district's starting point in the process.

Why so long?

It's important to understand the kind of change that you are leading.

What Kind of Change Is It?

The industrial-era model of change management taught us that implementing change was a linear process. This linear process took the form of a group of senior leaders gathering around a boardroom table for several meetings to explore, discuss, and decide upon the strategic priorities of the organization. These priorities were then shared with the broader community, ideally resources were assigned, a solid communication plan was implemented to ensure that everyone understood the changes, and change would occur as per the timeline in the strategic plan.

There are (very) few circumstances when this linear approach to change does work, but if you are leading the shift away from the industrial model of education, it is woefully inadequate to the task at hand.

In their 2009 paper, *Building Organizational Change Capacity*, Anthony Buono and Ken Kerber unpack the complexity of change and invite us to think about three different kinds of change (see Figure 2.2).

Figure 2.2 • What Kind of Change Is It?

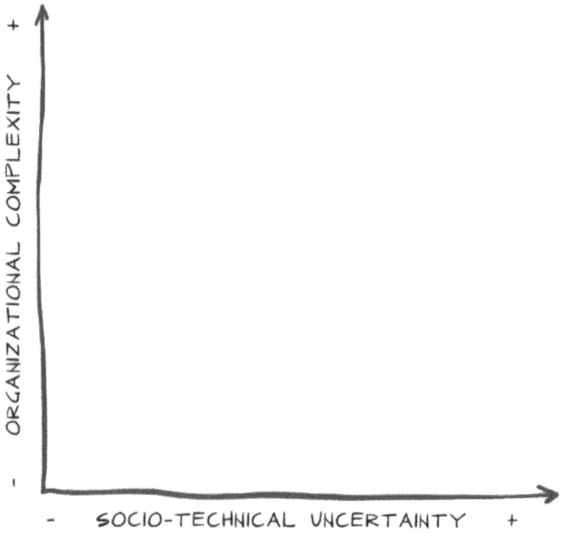

Source: Adapted from Buono & Kerber (2009). Illustration by Kelvy Bird.

There are two major factors to consider when identifying the kind of change you are leading and choosing your appropriate change strategy:

> **Organizational Complexity** (vertical axis) refers to the intricacy of the system in which the change is to be implemented. Factors include organizational size, the number of services or programs

offered, the extent to which different departments depend on each other for resources, and team interdependence to achieve desired results. The degree of complexity increases the more a change cuts across different departments and hierarchical levels, involves high levels of team interdependence, affects a range of services or programs, and requires the buy-in and support of a wide range of internal and external stakeholders. If we refer back to Figure 2.1 earlier in this chapter, we can see that moving from an industrial model of education to a postindustrial model checks all the boxes of high Organizational Complexity.

Socio-Technical Uncertainty (horizontal axis) refers to the quantity and type of information processing and decision making required to implement the change. This is "based on the extent to which the tasks involved are determined, established or exactly known" (Buono & Kerber, 2009). Again, referring to Figure 2.1, if I am working in a traditional school and I want to shift from "Time-Based Learning" to "Mastery-Based Learning," there is no cookie-cutter model for me to pull off the shelf and implement. It involves an iterative cycle of working through what I "don't know I don't know" and a considerable amount of outreach, research, mini pilots, and learning by doing. When the solution and implementation plan are clear, uncertainty is very low. When the solution and implementation plan require iterative cycles of testing and feedback, uncertainty is high.

Three different types of change emerge at the intersection of these two axes (see Figure 2.3).

Figure 2.3 • **Three Different Kinds of Change: Directed Change**

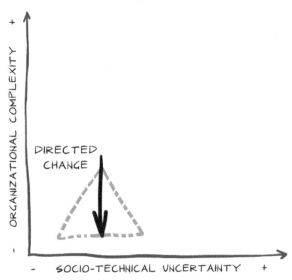

Source: Adapted from Buono & Kerber (2009). Illustration by Kelvy Bird.

Directed Change
(Low Organizational Complexity, Low Socio-Technical Uncertainty)

This is the kind of change that is low from both an organizational complexity and socio-technical uncertainty perspective (Figure 2.3). For example, a school district decides to change the physics textbook from version 11 to version 12 and mandates the change districtwide. The process to roll out a new textbook is known, the people who will lead the roll-out are readily identified, and the textbook provider likely has several supports in place to orient teachers toward the features of the new textbook. If a change such as this involves well-known and well-accepted actions in an environment that has the existing systems and processes in place, then directed change is often the most efficient and cost-effective approach. To be effective, this approach also requires a well thought-through communication plan describing the rationale and benefits of the change.

Planned Change
(High Business Complexity, Low-Medium Socio-Technical Uncertainty)

Many superintendents and principals are familiar with the process of planned change (Figure 2.4). Given the inherent complexity of a typical school or school district, many change initiatives follow a planned-change

Figure 2.4 • Three Different Kinds of Change: Planned Change

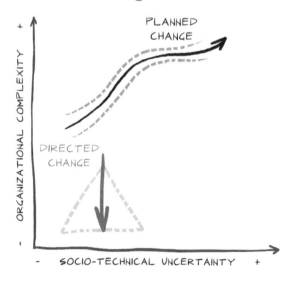

Source: Adapted from Buono & Kerber (2009). Illustration by Kelvy Bird.

approach. When it is critical that a large number of diverse stakeholders (i.e., teachers, administrators, students, parents, school board members, and community members) buy in to the change and support its implementation, a planned approach is needed. The planned approach requires input from key stakeholders in the planning process and strong project management skills. Helping the community get clear on the *why* of the change, what success will look like, the timeline of activities to implement, a thorough risk analysis, and a solid communication plan are critical components of planned change. Many school and district strategic planning processes follow this approach. The first year might involve a series of community meetings and focus groups, with multiple revisions of priorities by the community and school board. The second year begins the process of implementation and ongoing communication. The more participative the planning process is (by key stakeholders and the ultimate implementers of the change), the higher the chances of the change being sustainable. Implementation may be ongoing over several years.

Iterative Changing

(High Business Complexity, High Socio-Technical Uncertainty)

This is the land of "You don't know what you don't know." Iterative changing (Figure 2.5) is required when the tasks and processes to implement the change are unknown. Iterative changing requires experimentation and the willingness to fail. One of the biggest distinctions between planned

Figure 2.5 • **Three Different Kinds of Change: Iterative Changing**

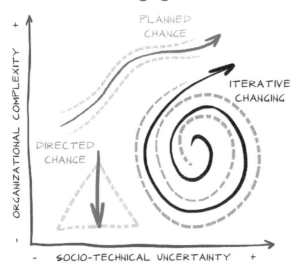

Source: Adapted from Buono & Kerber (2009). Illustration by Kelvy Bird.

change and iterative changing is that the change problem itself is unclear. It requires improvisation and learning and is an ongoing and emerging process, which is why we refer to it as *iterative changing* and not *iterative change*. For example, a superintendent who was leading a districtwide initiative to begin assessing the 4Cs (communication, creativity, critical thinking, and collaboration) experienced a combination of both planned change and unexpected iterative changing. He convened a group of teachers to begin the work of designing rubrics to assess the 4Cs across elementary, middle, and high school levels. Shortly thereafter, he noticed a lot of resistance from the teachers in the group who had volunteered for the task. When he inquired into the nature of the resistance (rather than just pushing back or ignoring it), he discovered that the majority of the district teachers did not know how to design a rubric. The problem was deeper than not having the tools to implement a new kind of assessment; the problem was a lack of assessment literacy across the faculty body. This iterative cycle of keeping an open mind with an appetite to discover and solve the real problem resulted in a very well-received series of professional development sessions on mastery-based assessment—development that provided a strong foundation to begin the work of building useful and practical assessment tools.

Iterative changing involves giving the work back to the people, knowing that it is up to the people who will implement the change to wrestle with the problem(s) they are trying to solve. This is a significant shift from the patriarchal or matriarchal model of school where the principal or superintendent will tell you what the problem is and, in many cases, provide the solution. It requires facilitative change leadership. As a principal, you might convene a group of teachers and administrators to ask them what is going well and what could be improved with the current change initiative. If the conversation stops there and you take all of the "things that could be improved" on your shoulders to fix, you have just lost a great opportunity for the group to learn and to build the capacity to solve their own problems.

Directed change, planned change, and iterative changing are all tools in your change leadership toolkit. If you are leading the change from an industrial model of education to a postindustrial model, the bulk of your work lies in the area of planned change and cycles of iterative changing. Change in this zone of iterative changing often means you are participating in an evolving and emergent field. Take assessment. Shifting from a standardized model of assessment to an assessment model that aims to measure the capabilities, skills, knowledge, and habits of mind of each student is a nascent field. EDUCAUSE launched its Assessment for Learning Project grant in 2015. Its explicit goal was to convene a number of grantees to build the field of alternative and meaningful assessments—because the field does not yet exist, it is being built as you read this. A change initiative aimed at assessing the skills outlined in Figure 1.1 (What's Worth Learning?) immediately puts you in the uncharted waters of iterative changing.

Differentiating Your Approach

Figure 2.6 is a summary of the three approaches to change: their characteristics, goals, process, leadership role, dynamics, and pace of change.

Oftentimes, the lines between these three types of change become blurred during the reality of the work. For example, you might start out with a visioning process (planned change) and then shift to forming teams of teachers, students, administrators, and parents to dig into the implementation of several workstreams, task forces, or design teams (iterative changing). These teams might go through six months to a year of rapid prototyping and feedback, testing what works and what doesn't. Once the data and feedback from these teams are distilled, recommendations might be made, for example, a major redesign of the school schedule, which might result in a mandate (directed change) that the schedule be changed to accommodate team-led, interdisciplinary, project-based learning. When you reflect on the different change methods available to you, think of a 3-D triangle of options as denoted in the figures and how you might shift from one to the other as the situation and goals suggest. Perhaps a planned

Figure 2.6 • Differentiating Approaches to Leading Change

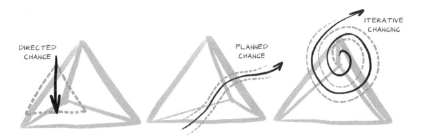

Dimensions	Directed Change	Planned Change	Iterative Changing
Characteristics	Top-down, hierarchical	Linear "roadmap"	Iterative spiral
Change Goals (Ends)	Tightly defined, unchanging goal	Clear goal, with some modification as needed	Loosely defined direction
Change Process (Means)	Tightly constrained	Flexible, participative	Experimental, improvisation
Change Leadership (Role)	Tell, order, command	Devise a plan to accomplish the goal	Point the way, guide and watch over, coach
Changemaker Dynamics	Persuasion	Influence, cooperation	Collaboration
Pace of Change	Urgent, fast, "just do it"	Go slow during planning to go fast during implementation	Act quickly, improvise, learn, react and continue to iterate

Source: Adapted from Buono & Kerber (2009). Illustration by Kelvy Bird.

change is not the way to go; perhaps it is more appropriate to run a series of pilots (iterative changing) to discover what is actually needed. Your context will help you decide the best way forward.

Stories From the Field

Leading Different Kinds of Change

Lourenço Garcia, Principal
Revere High School
Revere, MA

A great example of seeing different kinds of change in action is Revere High School (RHS) in Revere, Massachusetts. While Revere's school transformation started with a directed change, it is interesting to note how the principal led that directed change and then swiftly moved to planned change and iterative changing in order to shift the school toward the deeper learning he knew his students needed.

Lourenço Garcia joined Revere High School as its new principal in 2010. Prior to his arrival, there were great teachers at the school; however, the structure was not in place to support the vision that Lourenço had in mind for his students and the broader community. Specifically, the majority of the school's pedagogical and curricular practices leaned toward the industrial left-hand column of Figure 2.1.

When he became principal, Lourenço had a vision for personalized learning for every student in the school. He wanted students to have more time to delve into deeper work, to think critically, and to engage meaningfully with teachers in the process. As a new principal, he was tasked with leading a mandated change to transition the school from a traditional schedule of seven periods of forty minutes each to a four-block, ninety-minute schedule. Lourenço knew the research backed him up that a block schedule was the way to go; nevertheless, the community was skeptical:

I reached out to faculty. Every day would start with a headache. It went to a faculty vote and the vote was 51–49 in favor. We had a mandate, but a weak one. That was when I knew for sure I had to get people involved in the design and implementation of the work.

This is a great example of a directed change only getting the change leader so far. Lourenço had the mandate—but barely. He knew the essence of the work was not just to implement a new block schedule, but to equip teachers to become teacher leaders. The heart of the work for Lourenço was to shift from the top-down model of principalship to one of collaboration and shared decision making across the school's community.

He took a two-pronged approach: establishing professional learning groups (PLGs) and partnering with the best professional development providers he could find.

The PLGs were established to ensure horizontal as well as vertical curricular alignment from the elementary school through middle school and high school. Teachers started to meet within and across departments to look at student work and ensure there was coherence across grades and subject areas, and vertically at all levels.

Lourenço knew that the PLGs would require a solid structure and facilitation protocol to ensure they were productive. He provided the professional development and structure needed to set the teams up for success. Today, every PLG meeting has a designated facilitator. Each PLG sets its own norms and agenda and each month they submit monthly summaries of what has been discussed, tasks that have been completed, and outcomes that have been achieved. Lourenço and his team look at the themes that emerge and provide feedback. He admits that, yes, it is time consuming, but it is well worth it:

It reinforces teacher leadership. The job of a director is to empower teachers. It's all about sharing the work and empowering teachers to do the work. They are the experts. That's the way the school is run. It is run by the people who do the work—the teachers.

It takes time to build a culture of collaboration, shared decision making, and teacher leadership. Fast forward seven years to 2017 and every single teacher in Revere High School participates in at least one of twenty PLGs. These PLGs are an integral part of a broader support structure that sets the vision, direction, and its implementation at Revere.

An integral part of this structure (and I would argue a key element of the change process) is that every high school educator is a member of one of the teams or committees dedicated to continuing the work under way to improve student-centered learning at RHS—a great exemplar of iterative changing in action.

(Continued)

(Continued)

Leading this level of change requires courage, a steady focus, and a leadership ethos that believes in "leadership at all levels." As Lourenço notes, "It takes a village to transform a school," and this level of change requires sunsetting the old structures that no longer fit the vision (such as a traditional schedule), breaking down the silos of content and traditional disciplines, and embracing a model of shared decision making and distributed leadership. Lourenço is keen to ensure that development is ongoing and is mindful that anytime the school works with a consultant or professional development provider, the overarching model is that of "train-the-trainer" and building schoolwide capacity to take the work forward independently.

Conditions on the ground are always changing: refugees, demographics, financial downturns, funding levels. We capitalize on a train-the-trainer model—that's why we have so many emerging leaders in our school. It's all about empowering teachers and teacher leadership—making sure everyone shares the vision, communication is clear, and support and development are available.

Sustainable, meaningful change in high-need urban districts is too often thought to be an elusive goal. Revere High School proves that it can be done.

In this chapter, we explored the shifts that are needed when moving from the industrial model of education to a postindustrial model. These changes are not the kind of changes that can be led successfully only via directed change. If we want to move away from the industrial model of education and we want that change to be sustainable change, then cycles of planned change and iterative changing to build change leadership capacity are required. The heart of the work is not just "change management to get us through this one change," but rather building teachers' and administrators' capacity to lead and implement meaningful change on an ongoing basis.

Key Points

- The questions "What's Worth Learning?" and "How Is It Best Learned?" (Perkins, 2006) are inextricably linked; for example, a teacher cannot be expected to teach risk taking if students and teachers alike are not allowed to experiment and fail in the learning process.

- We learn best through hands-on interdisciplinary work, failure and trying again, exposure to mentors and guides, through story, through repeated practice with reflection and feedback, and by having the freedom to take risks.

- When a school goes through the process of identifying "What's Worth Learning?" the skills, knowledge, and habits of mind identified have tremendous impact on the pedagogical practices of the teachers who are charged with the design and facilitation of that learning.

- Deep culture change is required to change an existing traditional, industrial-era school or district into a flexible learning environment that prepares our children for an unknowable future.

- The shifts that need to take place when moving from the industrial model of education to a postindustrial model are illustrated below:

From	To
Students as passive recipients of content, exercising limited choice	→ Students as self-directed, entrepreneurial learners
Teacher as deliverer of content	→ Teacher as designer and facilitator of immersive learning environments
Little differentiation for student's individual strengths and interests	→ Strengths- and interest-based learning for every student
Time-based learning	→ Competency-based learning
Single discipline-based learning as curriculum driver	→ Interdisciplinary learning as curriculum driver
Learning grounded in static content and rote memorization of facts	→ Learning grounded in the real-world and practical application
Learning takes place on the school campus only	→ Learning takes place on campus and off campus, meaningful community and global partnerships
Content-based assessment via written tests or exams. Learning assessed by the teacher only	→ Mastery-based assessment of skills, knowledge, and habits of mind. Assessment by self, peers, teachers, and external experts

- Realistically, this level of change can take anywhere from five to seven years, depending on your school or district's starting point in the process.

- Directed change, planned change, and iterative changing are different change strategies—know which one you are choosing and why. If you are leading postindustrial school change, you will lead cycles of planned and iterative changing.

- Instead of thinking of this work as leading a singular "change," think of it as building organizational change capacity.

Questions for Reflection and Action

- Reflect on the skills, knowledge, and habits of mind that your school or district has identified as your North Star. How are they best learned? Is there a shared understanding among your faculty and is that understanding practiced?

- How might pedagogy shift in your school or district to support the learning outcomes you seek?

- How might that shift in pedagogy impact your culture? How might behavior and beliefs need to change?

- Refer to Figure 2.1; where on the continuum is your school or district today? Where would you like it to be one, three, or five years from now?

- Reflect on past change initiatives; what kind(s) of change were they (i.e., directed, planned, or iterative)? What worked well when helping to build organizational change capacity? In hindsight, what might you have done differently?

- Reflect on a current change initiative; what kind of change is it? How does this kind of change impact your change strategy moving forward?

- What additional questions did this chapter prompt for you?

- What action items did this chapter prompt for you?

Notes

" Always remember that the future comes one day at a time. **"**

—DEAN ACHESON

Chapter 3

FIVE SUCCESS FACTORS FOR CHANGE

In addition to building organizational change capacity, there are a number of success factors that support and help build that capacity to change. When changing a system, there are many moving parts to consider. While every school or district is unique, I have noticed over time that there are several distinct success factors that are critical if you are leading change from the industrial model to a postindustrial model. Think of these success factors as jigsaw puzzle pieces that need to be in place in order to support the change you seek.

Success Factor 1: Sustained Leadership and a Visionary School Board

Realistically, large-scale, sustainable change in schools or districts takes anywhere from five to seven years to implement, depending on the foundation that is already in place. This level of change requires a principal or superintendent who will commit to the timeframe necessary for the work and who will embrace the highs and lows of adaptive change (Heifitz et al., 2009). It also requires support from the school board as the leader navigates the organization through the highs and lows of change. Too often, visionary change is not realized because of leadership turnover with no succession planning in place to continue the work in a sustainable way. It can take years to see change happen and only a few months to undo.

Changing a school or district from a traditional industrial model requires not just visionary leadership, but leaders who will be there to coach, guide, and support deep implementation. The work I mentioned earlier at Revere High School (RHS) was supported by visionary, consistent leadership. As of this writing, Dianne Kelly, district superintendent, is a twenty-plus-year veteran of Revere public schools; she has occupied several roles during her tenure, including math teacher, STEM director, dean of students, and assistant superintendent. Her predecessor, Paul Dakin, was superintendent for fourteen years. Lourenço Garcia, the current high school principal, has been in his position for seven years. Lourenço was brought in from the outside to lead ambitious change at the high school in 2010. Since Lourenço joined RHS, the school went from a low-performing school as classified by the Massachusetts Department of Education in 2009 to winning the 2014 High School Gold Award at the National Center for Urban School Transformation (NCUST) conference in San Diego. The school also ranked Silver on the *U.S. News and World Report* survey of the best U.S. high schools and was awarded the 2016 School of Opportunity award (Gold Medal) by the National Education Policy Center. On any given day, twenty-seven languages are spoken at the school. The student body comprises 54.1 percent Hispanic/Latino, 32.7 percent White, 6.2 percent Asian, 4.7 percent African American, and 2.2 percent multirace non-Hispanic; 80 percent of students are on free or reduced lunch. Is consistent leadership the only success factor in this diverse urban school? No, but I would argue sustainable, meaningful change requires consistent leadership to see a vision through to implementation.

In addition to consistent school leadership, a school board has a critical role during change. The board's role is to support the move away from the industrial, factory-based model and to continue supporting the change when things get messy—and things will get messy. Any large-scale change takes an organization through a predictable cadence of "uninformed optimism" (Conner, 2006) during the honeymoon period when folks are excited about the change and possibilities, and then invariably a transition into "informed pessimism" (Conner, 2006) when the messiness of the change becomes explicit and the organization begins to resist the change. Opponents to the change become vocal, plans don't go as planned, and it may seem like the wheels are starting to come off the bus. The organization that was run according to principles of control and risk mitigation is now being introduced to creativity and the need to embrace risk. This kind of change requires the school board to take the long-term view, support its leaders, and understand the distinctions between directed change, planned change, and iterative changing. In many cases, the school board is building its own capacity to change while the school or district is building its capacity to change. In Chapter 4, I share a number of resources to help you start the conversation and lead the process of building change capacity.

Success Factor 2: A Shared Vision of the Change

A vision that has been generated by the community inside and outside the school or district requires a shared understanding of *why* things need to change and *what* needs to change as a result. This vision needs to be readily understood, agreed upon, and supported by the school board, teachers, parents, students, and community members. The goal is not that 100 percent of your community is in agreement (100 percent consensus for a group of that size is unlikely), but rather that you have clarity on the big themes that are important so that your school or district can get to work on its implementation, knowing that the vision has a broad level of support and understanding. When you are transitioning from the industrial model, ideally your visioning work should answer those four questions (Perkins, 2006) referenced earlier:

- What's worth learning?

- How is it best learned?

- How can we get it taught that way?

- How do we know it has been learned?

This visioning process can take anywhere from six to eighteen months. It cannot be done effectively if it is done quickly and in a vacuum. If you do it quickly and in a vacuum, you will have a vision, but you will look around and find little in the way of sustainable support for its implementation. This process not only establishes the vision but begins the process of changing the conversation and identifying your allies and supporters.

Once you have completed the visioning process, the work of implementation begins. Visioning and implementing change is like running a marathon. The visioning process gets you to the starting line of the marathon—you still have the implementation race, that is, the marathon, to run.

Once the visioning process is completed, do not underestimate the value of continually reminding the community of the *what* and *why* of the vision. When I asked Jared Cotton, superintendent of Henry County school district (Virginia), if there was anything he would do differently when leading change in his district, he said yes: he would have spent more time on the vision:

> When I arrived at Henry County, the vision was already in place. I assumed because the vision was in place that people were on board with it. The vision had all the right words, but people had not necessarily bought into it. I realized that many people did not have an understanding of what it meant. In hindsight, I should have spent more time with people on the vision—helping them understand the intent behind the words, the need for the change, and what success would look like. Now our vision and strategic plan are a living document. Each principal and central office administrator work on a goal related to the vision each year. We meet monthly and twice per year on extended retreat. We hold each other accountable to the vision and we connect every budget request to it. As a result of this work, we changed the vision—and now it's a living dynamic document.

Jared's previous comments are a great litmus test for your vision. One year, two years, five years later, is your vision a "living dynamic document," or has it gone to "binder heaven" on your fifth bookshelf, with no changes evident in student outcomes? Ensure your visioning process is a community effort and bring people along with you to implement and adapt as you go.

In Chapter 4, I share a number of tools and resources to help you begin and sustain the process of visioning in an engaging and human-centered way.

Success Factor 3: Unleashing Talent and Building Teams

Implementing a postindustrial vision means transitioning from the compliance and control model of education to one of agency and creativity. It requires embracing risk, and in many traditional schools, this is a 180-degree change from how teacher roles were conceived in the industrial model. In order to support the implementation of the vision, teachers need much more autonomy over the design and facilitation of learning and the evaluation thereof. It requires the formation of teacher teams to codesign classes, evaluate student work, observe each other's practice, coach, and give feedback. Job-embedded professional development and support is critical. A school or district vision will be implemented in direct correlation to teachers being given the autonomy and support to lead its implementation. It requires the fundamental shift from teacher as deliverer of prescribed content to teacher as lead learner and change agent.

Depending on where your school or district falls on the industrial→ postindustrial continuum, this might take a year or two, or it might take many more. How long it will take depends on a number of factors; perhaps the most significant factor is the level of trust in the school or district. Unfortunately, there are schools and districts that are operating under a leadership model of micromanagement with very low levels of trust. It is exceptionally difficult, if not impossible, to lead sustainable, meaningful change in an environment of low trust. If you find yourself in such an environment, your number one job is to start building trust.

Stories From the Field

You Need to Build Trust to Lead Change

David Miyashiro, Superintendent
Cajon Valley Union School District
El Cajon, CA

David Miyashiro, superintendent of Cajon Valley Union School District, describes his experience of becoming superintendent of a district that had previously operated with very low levels of trust. In his first six weeks as superintendent visiting schools in his district, he discovered that the teachers were in compliance mode and teaching toward fixed assessments. Teachers were on edge when leadership visited their classrooms with a checklist.

They were quick to tell David that posting every objective on the board did not have an impact on student learning and motivation. These classroom visits felt like "gotchas with a checklist." David saw immediately that he needed to take action and began creating an environment where people would feel safe.

If I had advice for a superintendent wanting to build trust in his or her district, I would say put 25,000 miles on your car. Go everywhere and meet everyone. Let people unload their frustrations. It's very cathartic and there was a relief that people felt heard and listened to. I asked a lot of questions. I let people share what they were frustrated about and what they were hopeful about. I didn't wait to take action once I heard the themes of what needed to change. In the first six weeks, I cancelled all the assessments that weren't helping the process of learning. If you're going to listen, you have to act. That first action gave me a lot of credibility.

David focused on team building, culture, and making the teachers' lives better. He did not force mandates; new initiatives were by invitation. For example, he offered an opportunity for teachers to work on a new blended learning initiative, sharing some research and asking teachers to make recommendations and design a plan—with the stipulation that they would have to commit to being a team. David notes what happens when you treat teachers with respect:

We had 90 percent of our teachers apply to be a part of that. When you give teachers the dignity and respect they deserve, you will get great results.

David has been in his role now for five years. Is everything perfect? No. He received as much criticism as he did praise and the work is ongoing, but he believes that when a teacher sees something that is good for kids, that teacher will change—and that you have to find these "beacons" in your district and celebrate the successes. For example, the fourth-grade team was collaborating effectively with each other and changing pedagogy. David brought in high-quality video crews and made this collaborative work public to the entire community. Unleashing talent and highlighting successes has a cumulative effect in building pride and trust.

In Chapter 4, we will explore practical tools to help you unleash talent in your school or district and build effective teams to implement the vision.

Success Factor 4: Rethinking the Use of Time and Space

The industrial model has dictated the physical set-up of classrooms and the school schedule, and for many schools, the use of space and time has not changed much in the last one hundred years. Once a school has established its vision and begins the work of curricular, pedagogical, and assessment redesign, the constraints of the schedule and the space of the traditional classroom quickly become apparent as obstacles to deeper change.

There is no singular model to follow when it comes to redesigning space and the schedule. It is important to start with the curricular and pedagogical priorities first, before rethinking and redesigning the use of time and space. When it comes to the schedule, you will likely find that you will pilot a number of different schedules to fit the community's needs. I worked with one school that decided to change the start time for the high school to a later time given the compelling research that teenagers need more sleep. The school was focusing on transitioning its approach to focus on the whole child—a schedule change was just one part of a larger pedagogical change and was supported by many programs, including helping students and parents understand the impact of sleep on developing teenage brains and the learning process.

Rethinking space can open up a host of possibilities; again, your North Star, or vision for your school or district, should help lead the decision making. David Miyashiro's vision for his district is simple: "Kids who are happy, healthy and engaged in their community." The district, along with the city, want to make El Cajon the best place to live and raise a family. By listening to his stakeholders, David discovered that the schools had contentious relationships with the city. He began to think about how he might use space to build community relationships:

Schools have playgrounds, cafeterias, multipurpose rooms—and we shut them down most evenings and over the weekend; we decided to open these up. We gave the local police department access to our buildings and sports fields for training. We connected with the church, the city, and local businesses and made our space available. It has helped to build much closer community relationships. We have an annual TEDx event for our kids and the entire community comes out in support—not just kids and their parents, but firefighters, police officers, and local business people.

We will explore tools and strategies to help you align time and space with your North Star in Chapter 4.

Success Factor 5: Overhauling the Assessment Structure of Learning and School Performance

Standardized testing, for the most part, actively reduces a child's intrinsic motivation to learn and is a blunt measure of a child's capabilities and potential. We need to start measuring what we truly value while understanding the reality that what gets measured, often results in unintended and negative consequences for the overall learning process. Measuring skills and habits of mind is a nascent field. If we say we want our graduates to be creative problem solvers, how do we assess that? How do we assess creativity and collaboration?

I believe assessment is an exceptionally powerful lever in the systems-level work of transforming the traditional factory model of education. Let me explain.

You may have seen this model before; it is an amended version of Geoffrey Moore's "Crossing the Chasm" model from a book by the same title wherein he explains why some technology gets adopted by the masses, while other technology does not (see Figure 3.1).

Figure 3.1 Crossing the Chasm

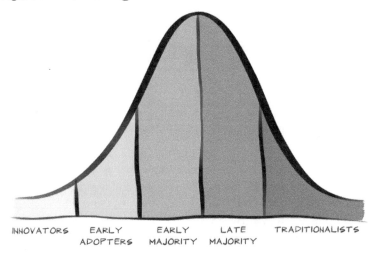

INNOVATORS   EARLY   EARLY   LATE   TRADITIONALISTS
              ADOPTERS   MAJORITY   MAJORITY

Source: Used by permission from Geoffrey A. Moore's *Crossing the Chasm*, 3rd Edition. Copyright © 1991, 1999, 2002, 2014 by Geoffrey A. Moore. Illustration by Kelvy Bird.

This model is often used as a tool to help explain why change initiatives might succeed or fail and helps us understand how we might support transformation efforts when wider spread adoption is needed. When I read Moore's (2014) book, it was through the lens of "How might this model help me understand changing the industrial system of education?"

Briefly stated, Moore's model tells us that the reason why so many change efforts fail is due to the chasm that exists between the early adopters and the early majority. One of the biggest differences between these populations is appetite for risk. Early adopters will adopt whatever the "it" is because their gut is telling them it makes sense to do so. They move on instinct and act in absence of proof. The fact that it has not been done before is reason enough to do it. In direct contrast, the early majority *requires* proof. They require evidence and incontrovertible data that "it" works before taking action.

Mapping sample progressive education practices on the model reveals that we are at an exciting juncture in education (see Figure 3.2).

Figure 3.2 • Crossing the Chasm: Mapping Progressive Education Practices

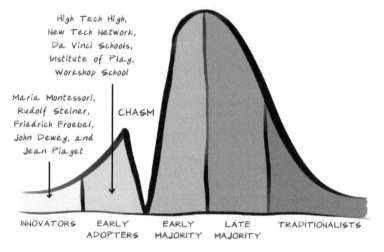

Source: Used by permission from Geoffrey A. Moore's *Crossing the Chasm*, 3rd Edition. Copyright © 1991, 1999, 2002, 2014 by Geoffrey A. Moore. Illustration by Kelvy Bird.

I think of the progressive giants, innovators such as Maria Montessori, Rudolf Steiner, Friedrich Froebel, John Dewey, and Jean Piaget (to name just a few), as the pedagogical innovators. They led the way by observing children and how they learn and were driven by a model of education that was before their time—a model that promotes creative problem solving, global citizenry, emotional intelligence, and self-efficacy, all grounded in a "whole child" approach to learning.

Standing on the shoulders of these giants is the great work of many modern-day exemplar schools and organizations including the following:

High Tech High, www.hightechhigh.org

New Tech Network, newtechnetwork.org

Virginia Beach City Public Schools, www.vbschools.com

Institute of Play, www.instituteofplay.org

Workshop School, www.workshopschool.org

Center for Advanced Research and Technology (n.d.), cart.org

Catalina Foothills School District, www.cfsd16.org

Brightworks, www.sfbrightworks.org

However, I am convinced that if we do not focus on how to assess the learning, and make that evidence and data available to a broader audience, we will not see widespread adoption of a more progressive pedagogy throughout the public system.

In Chapter 4, you will find examples of exciting work under way to build this nascent and growing field of assessment.

Leveraging these five success factors for change will help support you in leading the change you want to see in your school or district. Before we turn to Chapter 4, where we will explore a number of strategies and resources to help you get started in implementing these five success factors, it is important to understand the context in which this work can best succeed. If you take just one thing away from this book, please take this:

Leading your school or district from the industrial-age model of education to a postindustrial model is developmental work. You will be successful in direct correlation to the extent to which you focus on the adult development task at hand.

Leading Transformative Change Requires Adult Development

In Chapter 2, we explored the importance of understanding the kind of change you are leading and the idea that the majority of industrial→postindustrial school change initiatives are grounded in cycles of planned and iterative changing.

This is important context because it helps us understand what the change journey is all about. It's about building capacity to change—on an ongoing basis. As the world around us changes with ever increasing speed, it is vital that our education system not only keeps pace, but ideally positions itself ahead of the curve. This requires us, the adults, to build the skills to launch, implement, and nurture change.

I used to believe that change was a golden opportunity for a school to lead and support adult development. I have not so much changed my mind as I have doubled down on the initial theory. I now believe that a school or district will never achieve the shift away from the industrial model of education until and unless it focuses relentlessly on the adult development task at hand.

What do I mean by that?

From Socialized Minds
to Self-Authoring Minds

This level of development is not just about training or attending professional development programs; this is about developing as human beings. In his book *In Over Our Heads*, Robert Kegan (2003) articulates three stages of adult development (or orders of mind): Socialized Mind, Self-Authoring Mind, and Self-Transformational Mind. Kegan's theory describes the way in which we make sense of our environment and our relationships; it describes our internal process of making sense of the world. Each stage builds on the one that went before. No one stage is any better than the other; instead we should ask ourselves if the demands of the task at hand fit with our current "order of mind," or are the demands asking us to develop beyond it. Here is a brief synopsis of each stage:

> **Socialized Mind**—If I am operating from a socialized mind, I am defined by the group. As a teacher, I would look to others to tell me that I am doing a good job. As a superintendent, if I have a contradictory opinion to that of my board, I will likely withhold those contradictory views and go along with the board's wishes. My sense of self-worth is dependent on the feedback and the views of the group. If I am working in a culture that aligns with my values, I will likely thrive; if I am working in a culture that does not align with my values, I will likely find myself "in over my head." In many ways, I am shaped by the expectations of my environment.

> **Self-Authoring Mind**—If I am operating from a self-authoring mind, I am more self-directed in my thoughts and actions. The school may have a particular approach they want me to follow as a teacher; if it aligns with my values, I will do it; if it does not, I might simply close my classroom door and teach the way that does align with my values. As a superintendent, I will argue openly and assertively with my board when our opinions differ. I am able to set and maintain boundaries and I know my own mind. I am able to explore the thoughts and feelings of others and to create my own views, independent of the group.

> **Self-Transformational Mind**—If I am operating from a self-transformational mind, I am aware of the limits of my thinking and viewpoints. While I may believe strongly in something, I know that my thinking will likely have holes in it; I know my worldview cannot encompass all things. I can hold the tension of contradictory thought and polarities and my sense of self is not dependent on holding strong to a particular view. If I am a teacher or a superintendent with self-transformational mind, it is more likely that I will embrace paradox, welcome contradictory views, and be ever mindful of the limits of my thinking and my decisions.

According to Kegan's research, the majority of adults today find themselves in the transition from socialized mind to self-authoring mind. He also points out that one stage of mind or consciousness is not "better or worse" than the other; what is important is to recognize and understand the demands of our external environment and to reflect on the complexity of consciousness that is needed in order to navigate it. For many people, the developmental demands of our modern culture are inviting us to grow beyond the cognitive and emotional skill set of socialized mind.

When I visit schools that are focusing on helping students be much more self-directed in their learning, I see them break from the norms of the industrial, socialized-mind model. I also see the adults doing the same. Many of us who work in education were raised in the old system. Many of us excelled in it. We followed the rules, got good grades, and went to college. We were "good at school." However, with the tectonic volatile, uncertain, complex, and ambiguous (VUCA) plates shifting, that socialized mindset is not going to help us build what is next. It does not help us embrace a larger version of ourselves—one where we are exercising more autonomy and self-direction in our work. It is probably one of the biggest opportunities of large-scale school change. **If we want an education system that helps students design, build, and live a life of their own choosing, then we must help the adults build the skills of agency, self-direction, and creative problem solving alongside the students.**

Moving Away From the Patriarchal Model of Education

At its core, the rapidly accelerating pace of change is inviting us to shift from a socialized-mind industrial model of education to a more self-authoring postindustrial model of education. Our developmental task is to lead ourselves and not to depend on the patriarchal structure of institutions that were designed over a century ago. This requires deep culture change—change that recognizes the developmental task at hand, that is, that we are embarking on long-term work to transition a system that was designed along the principles of compliance and control, to become much more autonomous and creative.

This challenge was brought home to me when I visited Skapaskolan, a middle school near Stockholm, Sweden. When I met with Christer Holger, the school head, he explained how he knew he could not build the school he wanted to build without a different kind of organizational structure and method of shared leadership. The school's curriculum and pedagogy is grounded in nurturing agency—for students and adults alike. Christer introduced me to one of the teachers, who described how the school's teachers are responsible for the running of the school as self-forming autonomous teams. She described how she was excited to work at the school because she wanted to help lead it. She also admitted that it was the most challenging job of her career so far because she had to learn what she stood for, why she stood for it, and how to work collaboratively with others while they worked out how to serve the learning needs of the students in a flexible way.

I recall the head of a lower school who was just two years into his new role as a leader. He was tasked with leading the redesign of the school's math curriculum, a curriculum that had not been changed in twenty years. He wanted to bring more critical thinking and self-direction to the work. When he gathered the teachers and told them that he would like them to take the lead in the redesign, he received a significant amount of push-back regarding participation. The theme of the resistance was "Why don't you just tell us what to do. Tell us what you want and we'll do it." Even his boss told him he was not being "leaderly" enough and that he should tell the teachers what to do. But this leader knew that the redesign of the curriculum was a means and not an end in and of itself. He knew that he needed to lay the groundwork for the teachers to wrestle with the thorny challenge of curriculum redesign and to build their capacity to change via the redesign process.

Kegan's model helped me understand one of the biggest developmental tasks of leading change from the industrial to the postindustrial model of education: We are asking adults to make the shift from the socialized mind of checklists, scripts, and pacing guides, to the self-authoring mind of having autonomy over the design and facilitation of interdisciplinary projects and playing an active role in the creation and implementation of school change.

Depending on where your school currently falls on the industrial→ postindustrial continuum, you may have less or more developmental work to lead. Earlier, I shared the story of David Miyashiro and his leadership of a school district where the trust levels had been historically low. He described the challenge of helping teachers make the shift from a patriarchal structure to one where he was inviting teachers to have more freedom and autonomy (i.e., to be more self-authoring):

> In year two, we decided to "shake the cage." Having opened the birdcage door to let those birds fly, we discovered that about half of the people wouldn't fly out. Many were comfortable in the cage. The things that people had previously complained about, for example, teaching to the test, some teachers kept doing it. We had to let them know it was safe to start doing something different and that we would support them as they tried something new. I realized that many of the teachers had not been asked to think for themselves for over a decade. There was real fear when we took away the old "safe" systems.

Not all schools or districts are at the extreme end of the continuum; however, teachers and administrators are under a lot of pressure not to fail—whether that be a local public school or the most prestigious private school—and we need to provide support to help people through this change where we, more often than not, are asking them to try something new and to step outside of their comfort zone.

I share this by way of context for the strategies and resources that follow in the next chapter. When you are leading people through change, and that change involves asking people to become more self-authoring, your strategies should bear that human developmental task in mind.

Key Points

- These five success factors help support and build capacity to change:

  1. Sustained leadership and a visionary school board
  2. A shared vision of the change
  3. Unleashing talent and building teams
  4. Rethinking the use of time and space
  5. Overhauling the assessment structure of learning and school performance

- This level of development is not just about training or attending professional development programs; this is about developing as human beings.

- The three stages of adult development (Kegan, 2003)—Socialized Mind, Self-Authoring Mind, and Self-Transformational Mind—describe the way in which we make sense of our environment and our relationships; they describe our internal process of making sense of the world.

- If we want an education system that helps students design, build, and live a life of their own choosing, then we must help the adults build the skills of agency, self-direction, and creative problem solving alongside the students.

- The rapidly accelerating pace of change is inviting us to shift from a "socialized mind" industrial model education to a more "self-authoring" postindustrial model of education. Our developmental task is to lead ourselves and not to depend on the patriarchal structure of institutions that were designed over a century ago.

- Depending on where your school currently falls on the industrial→ postindustrial continuum, you may have less or more developmental work to lead.

Questions for Reflection and Action

- When you reflect on the five success factors for change, which are most applicable to your current change initiative?

- How are you enlisting your board members as supporters and advocates, not only for the change, but also for the overall change process?

- How might you build teams around the work of envisioning the change and the co-creation and implementation thereof?

- What impact is the change having on the use of time and space? How might you involve teachers and students in pilot programs to experiment with alternate models?

- Does your school measure what it values? If not, how might you change that?

- Reflect on your school or district's professional development practices—to what extent do they support the change you seek?

- How might you support the development of your teachers and administrators through the process of change?

- What additional questions did this chapter prompt for you?

- What action items did this chapter prompt for you?

Notes

_____

_____

_____

_____

_____

_____

_____

_____

_____

_____

_____

_____

_____

_____

_____

_____

_____

_____

_____

_____

_____

_____

_____

_____

_____

CHAPTER 3

> **"**When it comes to change, I always say double your timeline and decrease the number of initiatives by half.**"**
>
> —SANDRA TRACH, PRINCIPAL

Chapter 4

LEADING YOUR ORGANIZATION THROUGH CHANGE: STRATEGIES

Success Factors in Action

The strategies that follow are grounded in the five success factors referenced in Chapter 3. I include real-life examples of how others have used these strategies where applicable and provide additional background and resources to help contextualize some of the concepts discussed.

As a reminder, the five success factors are

1. Sustained leadership and a visionary school board

2. A shared vision of the change

3. Unleashing talent and building teams

4. Rethinking the use of time and space

5. Overhauling the assessment structure of learning and school performance

Figure 4.1 • Reference Guide: Success Factors in Action

Use Strategy . . .	To Develop Success Factor . . .
1. Your Learning History	1, 2, 3
2. The Future: Where Would You Like to Go?	1, 2, 3
3. Building Organizational Change Capacity	1, 3
4. Helping Others Through Change—The Power of Development	3
5. It's a Marathon, Not a Sprint—Leading Through the Uncertainty of Change	2, 3
6. Building Effective Teams	3
7. It Could Be a Library or . . .	3, 4
8. Measuring What We Value	3, 5

As you can see from Figure 4.1, many of the activities have multiple applications. Choose whichever you find most helpful and amend to fit the needs of your own school or district.

Strategy 1: Your Learning History

Purpose: Provide a strong foundation for visioning work and collaboration by grounding the school and its community in the school's history and learning so far.

Resource: Figure 4.2, Learning History

In our rush to move forward, too often we ignore the lessons learned of the past. Taking time to remember the past and to share our collective history is an integral part of visioning.

I first learned of this work through The Grove, a group of graphic facilitators led by David Sibbet. David is a forty-year veteran of working with large-scale community-led change; he underscores in his work that change requires process, structure, and humanity in equal measure. The Learning History activity is one of my favorite tools because it honors the past and invites a group to learn from its shared history as it begins to design and create its future.

What is the history of your school or district? What is unique? What have you learned over the years? What do you want to carry forward?

We learn deeply through story and the learning history helps a community do just that. The learning history brings our past alive and honors the work that has gone before. A visioning process that does not take time to look back often has the unintended consequences of saying everything that has gone before is no longer valid and avoids the lessons learned from prior change initiatives. It invites the new people to learn from the veterans and it grounds the group in a shared understanding of history and of context. You cannot move people forward until you meet them where they are. This activity meets a group where it is—in a rich, fun, and meaningful way.

You can facilitate this process by sketching the illustration in Figure 4.2 on a wall chart or whiteboard and starting the conversation with the large group by asking them to note their input using words or phrases and drawings. Alternatively, you can distribute sticky notes and ask group members to note items before beginning the large group conversation.

Here are a few guidelines for what is typically included for each of the elements. It is helpful to begin the debrief from the ground up, that is, "Key Events," making your way up toward the top and capturing "Learning."

> **Learning:** What did the school, district, or team learn over the years? What have we learned about our school, district, and community? How might we leverage that learning as we begin to envision what we want to build moving forward?

Figure 4.2 • Learning History

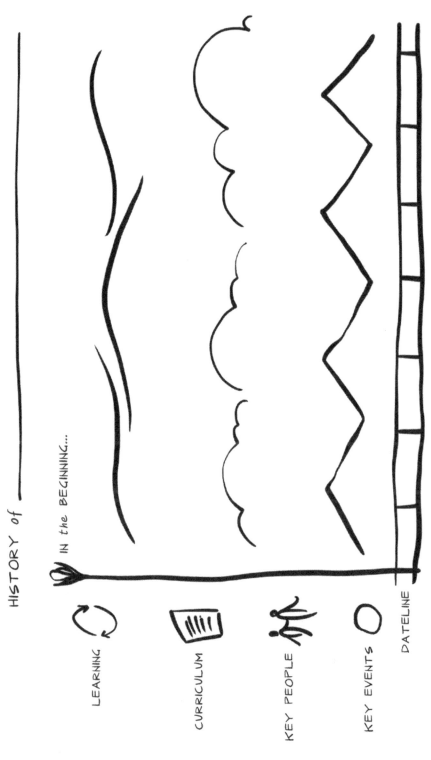

Source: Adapted from Graphic History, The Grove Consultants, 1996. Illustration by Kelvy Bird.

Curriculum: How has the curriculum morphed and changed over the years? This can be an especially rich discussion; perhaps the school was leading project-based curriculum in the 1990s before the introduction of NCLB—and here we are, decades later, bringing it back!

Key People: Anybody related to the school community. Encourage participants to bring photographs to post in this section—they are a great addition to rekindle memories and spark discussion.

Key Events: Think broadly in scope—events could be building renovations, community key events, changes in pedagogy or technology, or leadership changes.

Dateline: You can pick whichever date suits the context of your work. It might be the start date of the founding of the school, this particular team, or project.

I have used this activity for groups of one hundred people (with wall charts sixteen feet wide on the gymnasium walls) and with small groups of a dozen or so people with a sketch of the Learning History on a whiteboard.

Bringing teachers, administrators, parents, board members, students, and community members into this conversation helps a school and its community ground in its history before moving forward toward the future. It honors the past and the veterans in the school community and provides a strong foundation to begin visioning work.

Strategy 2: The Future: Where Would You Like to Go?

Purpose: Generate a vision that begins the process of change in a sustainable, meaningful, and human-centered way.

Resources:

Key Elements That Support the Process of Sustaining Real Change

School Retool (n.d.), *Shadow a Student Challenge*

Douglas County School District (n.d.), Sample Strategic Plan and Progress Updates

Mount Vernon Institute for Innovation (2014, June), *DEEPdt Design Challenge Playbook*

Grove Consultants International (n.d.), *Graphic Planning Tools*

Peter Senge et al. (2012), *Schools That Learn*

Next Generation Learning Challenges (2017a), MyWays Project

EdLeader21 (n.d.), *Profile of a Graduate Campaign*

What is the vision for your school or district? Is it is a living, breathing document that impacts student and teacher learning, or is it a statement that resides on the "About Us" page of your school's website that bears no relation to what happens day to day?

In many ways, the traditional strategic planning process is grounded in industrial-age management models, hierarchy, and processes. If we want a more human-centered system of education, we need a human-centered way to build our vision, make decisions, and support people through the process of change.

How you start the process of change is critical. It sets the tone and models the new approach. Building a vision together starts the process of change. How do you do that in a meaningful way? There are any number of human-centric ways to lead a visioning process. Regardless of how you lead your own visioning process, there are three key elements that support the process of change in a way that promotes and sustains real change.

Key Elements That Support the Process of Sustaining Real Change

Your Visioning Process

1. **Includes the Representative Voices of Your Community**—An inclusive process that invites participants from a broad cross-section of the school's community, that is, teachers, administrators, board members, parents, students, and local community members. I remember facilitating a visioning session where the majority of the ideas that were brainstormed were quickly followed by "But I don't think the board will support that." It prompted me to always invite board members to any visioning session thereafter. I also recall a visioning session where the topic of assessment came up. One of the adult participants mentioned that the school should start measuring skills, in addition to content knowledge; immediately, another adult mentioned that the current report card already included skills such as collaboration. The conversation was about to move on, when a student said, "Yes, but that section doesn't matter." "Why not?" asked one of the adults. The student replied, "Because it's on the last page and in super-small font, compared to the subject grades, so we all assume it doesn't matter." Inviting students into the conversation ensures your visioning process is grounded in the reality of the student experience.

2. **Is Outward and Inward Looking**—A process that invites its participants to look at the internal past, present, and future of the school and, in equal measure, explores the realities outside the school walls from a social, economic, political, and technological perspective. Be sure to look at head data and heart data. Head

data includes political changes at the city, state, and federal levels (e.g., Every Student Succeeds Act [ESSA] legislation), technological advances (e.g., massive open online courses [MOOCs], apps, artificial intelligence, virtual reality), economic (e.g., globalization, the changing job market and nature of jobs), and societal (e.g., changes in student demographics). Heart data includes the reality of the student experience. A great example of this is shadowing a student for a day. You can download a free toolkit at shadowastudent.org (School Retool, n.d.). When teachers, administrators, principals, even board members, shadow a student for a day, it can yield profound insights. An administrator recently shared his experience shadowing a student for the day—going so far as taking the student's bus to and from school and carrying a backpack of similar weight and size. His insights included (in addition to the unreasonable weight of that backpack) the disjointed and rushed nature of going from one class to the next, the 5 a.m. wake-up call to get to the bus stop on time and feeling exhausted by lunchtime, the extraordinary number of worksheets and lack of being asked to think for himself during the day, and zero connections being made between subjects.

3. **Is Transparent and Well Communicated**—Your school's community knows the visioning process is happening, the purpose of it, and how the process is unfolding. They are invited to be part of it as creators and participants, not just as consumers. Preparatory materials are made available online, along with summaries of data generated and decisions made. It is important to continue documenting the work and sharing progress made as the journey unfolds—and to make it publicly available to remind the community of where you have been, where you are going, and highlighting progress made and lessons learned along the way. Here is a wonderful example of a transparent and well-communicated visioning process (and ongoing implementation progress updates) from Douglas County School District in Colorado (n.d., at https://www.dcsdk12.org/district/strategic-plan).

There are many resources available and ways in which you might structure and facilitate your visioning process. These are three of my favorite resources:

1. Mount Vernon Institute for Innovation (2014, June), *DEEPdt Design Challenge Playbook* (a free download can be found at www.mvifi.org/designthinking)

2. The Grove Graphic Planning Tools (found at www.grove.com)

3. *Schools That Learn* by Peter Senge, Nelda Cambron-McCabe, Timothy Lucas, Bryan Smith, Janis Dutton, and Art Kleiner (2012) (found at www.schoolsthatlearn.com)

4. Next Generation Learning Challenges (NGLC, 2017a), *My Ways Toolkit* (free, research-based tools—includes customizable community presentation slides, activities to define success and design learning, and current case studies, found at https://myways.nextgen learning.org)

Here are just three sample exercises that can help the group establish the vision in a meaningful way. Each exercise builds on the one that went before and the preceding work with the Learning History.

Exercise 1: What Does Great Learning Look Like in Action?

The heart and soul of any school is learning. This is where visioning starts. By simply asking the group the question "What was your most impactful learning experience?" we get to the core of the work quickly.

Distribute sticky notes and ask the group to reflect on their most impactful learning experience in their life to date. Give participants a few minutes to reflect and recall that experience. It can be inside or outside the formal school or college environment. Ask the group to note their experience on a sticky note.

Then ask the group to reflect on why it was an impactful experience and to share that experience with at least two other people and to learn the experience of at least two other people.

Debrief the key takeaways—what are the themes?

Exercise 2: What's Worth Learning?

Exercise 1 can be followed by the "What's Worth Learning?" question referenced in Chapter 1. Following the same process as before, ask the group, "What should our students know and be able to do as young adults? How do we know?" Follow the same sticky note-generation activity and sharing with others process, as noted before.

A "live" research project can also be a great way to help the group dig deeper. During the meeting, you can divide the group into teams and give them questions to research in forty-five to sixty minutes and compile a "rough and ready" flip chart or two describing their findings. Potential questions you might include are the following:

*   What does our entering class of students need to know and be able to do to be successful young adults?

*   What are the current and anticipated education policies that will impact our work for the next three to five years?

- How have jobs changed in the last ten years? What will the world of work look like a decade from now?

- What are the top five technological advances that will impact education three, five, or ten years from now?

- How does globalization impact the world our students will live in as young adults? How does it impact them now?

- How have our student demographics changed in the last ten years? How might they change in the next ten years?

Follow the research section with a gallery walk and debrief key takeaways.

Exercise 3: *Time* Magazine Pays a Visit, or NBC, or the *Wall Street Journal*, or . . .

Ask the group to imagine it is five years from today and the school has achieved national recognition for its work. This can be in the format of a national newspaper, magazine, or a *60 Minutes*–style TV show. Why has the school achieved national recognition for its work? Divide the large group into subgroups and ask them to begin brainstorming ideas. The goal with brainstorming is quantity, not quality; do not censor ideas at this stage. Encourage the group to think big. After fifteen minutes or so, encourage groups to check out the ideas of other groups and then return to their own groups to share additional ideas and shortlist their one big idea. Note these on a flipchart and ask each group to present their ideas. What are the themes? What distinguishes the school five years from now? Why is that important?

Pulling It All Together

Be sure to capture all of the sticky notes and commentary throughout this process and upload to a shared space such as Dropbox or Google Drive. You will refer back to these documents and artifacts regularly as the process unfolds.

These are just three sample exercises. The type of exercise does not matter so much as the endpoint you will reach. Ideally your exercises, questions, and overall process will give you the community's answers to "What's Worth Learning?" and "How Is It Best Learned?"

Now it is time to take the group's collective input and draft your vision statement. I like to call this statement the school's North Star. You might have "Portrait (or Profile) of a Graduate" or different framing. (You can access free resources from EdLeader21 to help build a Profile of a Graduate at http://profileofagraduate.org.) This vision statement will guide the school's curricular, pedagogical, and resource allocation decisions in the immediate future and in years to come. Ideally one or two people will draft the vision and run it by various stakeholder groups for input and amendment. Wordsmithing a vision statement in a committee is rarely a helpful process—better for one or two people to take the lead on this.

Having established your North Star, you have started the process of change. Now it is time to begin the work of implementing the change and leading your organization through the change process.

Strategy 3: Building Organizational Change Capacity

Purpose: Identify priorities to begin the process of building organizational change capacity.

Resource: Organizational Change Capacity Questionnaire (Appendix)

In Chapter 3, we explored three different kinds of change (directed, planned, and iterative) and the importance of building change capacity. The "Organizational Change Capacity Questionnaire" in the Appendix is an accompaniment to that framework and is a great tool to use with your board, faculty, and leadership team. Simply ask your team to complete the questionnaire ahead of your next meeting and debrief the results. You will find sample debrief questions at the end of the questionnaire. Visit the book's website at www.the-IFL.org/TheHumanSide to download an electronic copy of the questionnaire.

The questionnaire starts a conversation regarding the need to build change capacity on an ongoing basis, as defined by the following dimensions:

- Facilitative Culture
- Supportive Infrastructure
- Different Change Approaches
- Ongoing Strategizing
- Sufficient Resources
- Willingness and Ability to Change

By identifying the high priority dimensions, you can begin making decisions on which priorities you will focus, and the work that is needed to increase your school or district's change capacity. Your resulting decisions will then become an integral part of the strategic plan.

Strategy 4: Helping Others Through Change—The Power of Development

Purpose: Begin the process of developing people through change.

Resources:

Individual Development Plan (Appendix)

The Strengths-Based Conversation (Appendix)

Gallup (n.d.), Strengths Assessment

VIA Institute on Character (n.d.), Character Strengths

Each school or district has its own unique starting point when changing from the industrial model of education to a more personalized, interdisciplinary, knowledge and skill-based model. Whatever your starting point, you are not gathering teams to implement the work and check it off a to-do list. Instead, you are building the capacity for your teachers, administrators, and students to be active participants in building what is next. You have started the process of building a true learning organization. You are building the capacity for your school and its community to change. This is one of the biggest shifts for a school grounded in an industrial-era model administrative structure. At its core, this work invites the school to move from a system of control and compliance to one of autonomy and creativity. This takes time, patience, and tolerance for ambiguity.

"How do we help others through change?" might be one of the least asked questions in education today. There is much talk of innovation and the need for change, but little in the way of how we might help ourselves and each other through the uncertainty, doubt, and fear of failure as we embark on the path of change.

This is the messy middle of change. It is that place where we have to let go of the old way and find ourselves in the liminal space in between the old and the new. At a macro level, this is where so many communities today find themselves with our schools. We know the old industrial model of school is no longer serving our children, yet the new way is in the process of revealing itself and there are no "right" answers; it is a time of experimentation, risk taking, and not knowing.

And that's a scary place for schools to be. The worst answer, in the majority of educational environments, is "I don't know." However, it's that tolerance of risk and embracing of ambiguity that is key for any school or district when implementing change. When we establish teams to get to work on the implementation of the North Star, we essentially immerse the teams in "not knowing." The way forward is rarely clear and it brings up a lot of questions.

Often these questions are viewed as resistance and obstruction. Sometimes they *are* obstructionist, but more often than not, if we dig deeper, these questions are not deliberately obstructionist, but rather reveal questions of genuine concern and a desire to know the right way forward.

When leading change, you have a choice. You can continue with the control, resist, increase the control doom spiral, or you can meet people where they are and start the process of increased autonomy and risk taking. It is simple and it is challenging. Not everyone will come on board. You will likely have your diehard resisters who will resist, just for the sake of resisting, but I find that this subgroup is rarely more than 10 percent of the entire group. One superintendent who is leading districtwide change noted that of his six hundred teachers, twelve (2 percent) have been actively working against the change for three years. While he finds it very challenging at times, he wisely concentrates his energies on the other 98 percent (588 teachers)—the teachers who believe in the change and who are committed to its implementation.

What works when leading others through change?

Developing people through this work is the rudder that will help steer the ship toward the North Star. Start with the people, their strengths, and how they can see themselves developing through this work. I have facilitated this process in many different environments; oftentimes, it is the first time that the teachers and administrators have thought about their strengths and how they might develop themselves through this process. I recall a school district that was in the middle of a turnaround. The state had taken over the district due to dysfunctional leadership and low performance. The new superintendent had insightfully identified teacher development as core to the turnaround—not teacher development as in "Let's double down on a teacher evaluation and an accountability plan," but teacher development as in "Let's unleash the potential of every single teacher in these buildings." We facilitated a session on *Strengths Based Leadership* (Rath & Conchie, 2009) and a draft roadmap of the work ahead, identifying what success would look like for each teacher by the end of the year, the skills they were developing, the challenges they might encounter, and how to overcome them. Several teachers noted at the end of the session that it was the first time they had been invited to think about what they were good at and how they wanted to develop their skills through this work.

One of the biggest shifts that you can lead is to begin focusing on the individual development of every adult involved in the change process. The Tilton School, a Grade 9 to 12 boarding school in Tilton, New Hampshire, has "Adult Self-Discovery" as one of the pillars of its change process. Tilton wisely recognizes that it cannot support the development of its students and ignore the development of its teachers and administrators. The school is in the process of realigning its recruiting, onboarding, and development processes to align with their North Star. Every employee has completed an Individual Growth Plan and identified personal strengths and explained how he or she will use those strengths in leading change at Tilton. This is a cultural shift and it will take time, but the more open and supportive this kind of process is, the more quickly the organization will build its capacity for change.

Exercise: Align Your People Development Practices With the North Star

How might you revise, or even overhaul, your existing employee development practices to support your North Star? Reflect on your school or district's goal setting, midyear review, ongoing coaching, and end of year processes—how might they be revised or redesigned to support the development of every employee toward the school or district vision? The heart of this work is shifting the annual goal-setting process from a check-the-box bureaucratic exercise to one that seeks to unleash the potential of every employee toward the vision inherent in the North Star—AND to help them navigate the process of change.

In the Appendix, you will find two tools to help you get started—a sample Individual Development Plan template to amend as you see fit, and a series of prompts for a strengths-based conversation. Additional tools include the Gallup (n.d.) Strengths Assessment, which you can purchase online at https://www.gallupstrengthscenter.com; alternatively you can access a free online strengths assessment from the VIA Institute on Character (n.d.) at https://www.viacharacter.org.

This work takes time. Depending on your school's current approach, it might take anywhere from one to three years to design, iterate, and embed a culture of meaningful development—development that moves the school's pedagogical and curricular vision forward.

Strategy 5: It's a Marathon, Not a Sprint—Leading Through the Uncertainty of Change

Purpose: Understand the distinction between change and transition and help others through ambiguity and uncertainty.

Resources:

Managing Transitions: Making the Most of Change by William Bridges and Susan Bridges (2017)

Figure 4.3, Ending, Neutral Zone, New Beginning

Figure 4.4, Ending, Neutral Zone, New Beginning—In an Ideal World

Figure 4.5, Ending, Neutral Zone, New Beginning—Reality

The 4Ps—Example

What's scary about this? What's scary is I don't know how to do this. I have been an effective teacher for seven years. I know my classroom; I know my curriculum; I know how to engage my students. I also know that I need to collaborate more with other teachers. I want to be more creative and give my students more autonomy. I want to work with them and to be the best teacher I can be. I want to open my classroom doors, invite other teachers in, and for them to give me feedback. But I'm scared. I'm scared to open the door.

—Teacher in a high school in the middle of change

The Bridges' model on *Managing Transitions* (2017) is one of my go-to resources in this work. Something as simple as providing a copy of the book for team members and discussing the process of change and the uncertainty of transition helps the group to build a shared vocabulary around the process of change and transition. The process of change is a marathon, not a sprint, and just as in a marathon, some folks are at the front running a fast pace to the finish line, others are struggling at the back, and many folks of differing levels of speed are in between. As the leader of change, you are probably out front to begin with. Part of your role is to switch from lead runner to coach. You are simultaneously setting the pace for the marathon while running up and down the length of the race helping runners run their own race.

In *Managing Transitions*, the Bridges discuss the difference between *change* and *transition*. Change is relatively quick and external to us, while transition is slow and is an internal process. Take moving your house as an example; it is a (relatively) quick process to pack boxes, load them onto a truck, and place them in your new house. However, the process of that new house becoming your home is a much slower and more gradual process. Change involves gain, while transition involves loss. Few people would argue that it is a good thing that students take part in a well-designed interdisciplinary project where collaboration, creative problem solving, and communication skills will be developed and assessed. However, if I have taught on my own for a number of years and have no experience designing or facilitating this kind of learning, I will experience a significant loss of competence and mastery. You are asking me to do something at which I may or may not be successful.

The Bridges talk about the Ending of transition, the New Beginning of transition, and the uncertainty of the Neutral Zone in between. Your job, as a leader of change, is to help your school and community manage the Endings and help them navigate through the uncertainty and learning inherent in the Neutral Zone (see Figure 4.3).

During the ending, we experience loss. In our Western world, we are not very good at managing endings. We are very keen to get onto the next new

Figure 4.3 • Ending, Neutral Zone, New Beginning

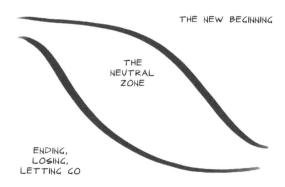

Source: Adapted from Bridges & Bridges (2017). Illustration by Kelvy Bird.

thing. With endings, we experience grief and disorientation. Perhaps a program is ending that you helped bring into existence, a new configuration of the school building is taking you out of the comfort of the classroom you have spent many hours making a welcoming space for your children, or a new schedule marks the ending of a well-known cadence to your week.

The Neutral Zone is the best of times and the worst of times. It is a period of ambiguity and uncertainty but also a time of learning and creativity. It is the liminal space between the old and the new and we often underestimate the power of this space in our desire to just push through it. This is a ripe time for pilots, trying new things, experimentation, and letting people know it is OK not to have all the answers. This is the chrysalis of change.

The New Beginning brings a sense of renewal and a welcome feeling of "We did it!" A feeling of competence returns and a sense of momentum and progress toward our goals materializes.

In an ideal world, we would move gracefully from the Ending, through the Neutral Zone, and happily into the New Beginning (see Figure 4.4).

Figure 4.4 • Ending, Neutral Zone, New Beginning—In an Ideal World

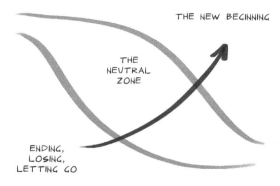

Source: Adapted from Bridges & Bridges (2017). Illustration by Kelvy Bird.

Realistically, it looks a lot more like Figure 4.5.

Figure 4.5 • Ending, Neutral Zone, New Beginning— Reality

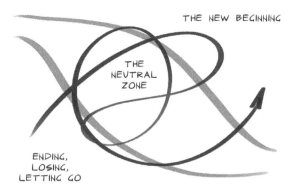

THE NEW BEGINNING

THE NEUTRAL ZONE

ENDING, LOSING, LETTING GO

Source: Adapted from Bridges & Bridges (2017). Illustration by Kelvy Bird.

As a leader of change, part of your role is to help others through this process; understanding it is not linear and it takes time.

Exercise: The 4Ps

The 4Ps (Bridges & Bridges, 2017) is a practical tool to help lead your organization through the uncertainty inherent in change and transition. It helps articulate where you are going, the necessity for the change, the plan on how you will get there, and how the community can participate. While it is highly unlikely you will experience a nice linear path through the Neutral Zone, these 4Ps will give you and your community guidance and direction. Use the questions below in a brainstorming meeting with your team or stakeholders and use the answers in ongoing communication efforts that support the change:

Problem—What is the problem you are trying to solve? Why is this change necessary? Define the need for the change.

Picture—What will success look like? What will it look like from the student, teacher, administrator, or parent perspective? Describe it in vivid detail and tailor it to each audience.

Plan—What is the plan to get from here to there? What are the milestones along the way and how will you know when you have reached them? Describe the steps to get there (and the extent to which they are known) and the need to be flexible.

Part—What part can your school community play in getting there? Let people know (teachers, administrators, parents, students, community members, etc.) how they are part of making the change happen. Invite people into the process; how can they be part of it?

The 4Ps are a great tool to draft, refine, and share as you lead your community through the ambiguity and uncertainty of change. Johnna Maraia, principal of Sanfordville Elementary School in Warwick Valley, New York, used the 4Ps as she led a schoolwide initiative to redesign their report card. Along with a team of teachers, she distilled the 4Ps as follows:

The 4Ps—Example

1. The Problem to be solved

   Our current report card is not aligned with the learning standards to which we are expecting our students to be accountable.

2. The Picture of Success will look like

   By September, we will have a Standards-Based Report Card that
   - assesses Writers' Workshop Skills
   - assesses 21st Century Skills (TBA)
   - includes more positive comments and/or narrative

3. The Plan will be
   - to meet monthly
   - possible July Meeting
   - to complete minor tweaks by June
   - to roll out at Superintendent Conference in September
   - Professional Development Training in October
   - to be prepared for Parent Conferences in November

4. The Part you will play—our roles
   - research—all
   - decision making—all
   - grade-level input
   - design—what it looks like
   - research rubric
   - assist with roll out

The 4Ps helped Johnna and her team stay on course and make significant progress in just nine months.

Strategy 6: Building Effective Teams

Purpose: Set teams up for success by understanding the predictable stages of development and working on the tasks required at each stage.

Resources:

The Five Dysfunctions of a Team, Patrick Lencioni (2002a)

Figure 4.6, The Four Stages of Team Development

Many teachers have begun the shift toward working as interdisciplinary, collaborative teacher teams and away from spending the bulk of their time designing curriculum and teaching alone. This is essential if we are to move away from silos of dislocated content toward a more holistic and integrated curriculum.

A great example of what is possible is the Center for Advanced Research and Technology (CART) school in Fresno, California. The CART curriculum combines rigorous academics with technical, design, process, entrepreneurial, and critical-thinking skills and is organized around four career clusters: Professional Sciences, Engineering, Advanced Communications, and Global Economics. These four clusters are shaped via sixteen interdisciplinary labs. The labs are team taught by three teachers and class sizes can hold up to ninety or so students.

When I spoke with teachers at CART, they underscored the importance of teacher collaboration and shared prep time. Typically teachers spend five to six hours per week in formal and informal collaborative prep time. These types of meaningful, interdisciplinary learning opportunities are simply not possible without collaborative teams and providing the time, space, and support to build them.

It takes time to build and sustain teams, and there are many resources out there that are helpful as teams work through the stages (Tuckman, 1965) of

- Forming—the honeymoon period
- Storming—when reality hits and conflict emerges
- Norming—building the skills to engage in productive conflict with agreed-upon norms of behavior
- Performing—full responsibility of team working toward shared purpose

One of my favorite resources is *The Five Dysfunctions of a Team* (2002a) by Patrick Lencioni. Several resources can be downloaded for free from his website www.tablegroup.com/books/dysfunctions. If the phrase *artificial harmony* resonates with your experience working on a team, you will find these resources helpful. Lencioni's theory is grounded in the fact that teams need to build the skills to have productive conflict. If two or more people are working together, it is inevitable they will have a difference in opinion—it is a guarantee. Therefore, we need to build the skills to have difficult conversation and engage in productive (not destructive) conflict. The key to being able to engage in productive conflict is trust. If I do not trust you, it is unlikely I will engage in conflict with you in a productive manner. Instead I might choose to avoid the topic altogether or talk about it indirectly and outside the room. Building trust is critical for teams and that involves coming out from behind ourselves into conversation, being vulnerable, and sharing what we think in a way that is respectful of our fellow team members.

The below exercise on Personal Histories (Lencioni, 2002b) is a simple way to begin the process of building trust on a team. It takes anywhere from 10 to 40 minutes depending on the size of the group and how long you would like to spend on it. It helps us get to know our colleagues as human beings, as we work on implementing our vision.

Exercise: Personal Histories [Amended from Lencioni, 2002b]

1. How many people are in your family and where do you fall in the birth order?

2. Share an interesting experience from your childhood.

Share the purpose of the exercise (i.e., to get to know each other and to build trust in support of the work ahead) and ask team members to share their answers to the above two questions. Each person takes five minutes or so to do so. This exercise is easy to facilitate and generates a great conversation. I have had many participants say that they have known some of their colleagues for years (sometimes decades) and learned more about them in a fifteen-minute Personal Histories conversation than they had in the preceding years.

Building trust takes time and concentrated effort. Depending on the current level of trust within your school or district, you may have more or less trust-building work ahead of you. Connecting the need for trust building with the curricular and pedagogical vision grounds it in the essential work of the school or district.

The change that Sandra Trach led in her school is an example of what is possible when you bring teams together—and the fact that it takes time and focus to help set teams up for success. Sandra established several teams during her tenure as principal; the first team she established was a leadership team to work on pedagogy. During her initial observations as a new principal, she had noticed that there were pockets of great practice at the school; however, two students in the same grade could be experiencing wildly different learning environments. Some classes were grounded in what Sandra knew were best practices as corroborated by the latest neuroscience, while others were more grounded in the industrial model of content dissemination and recall.

Sandra invited everyone who was a stakeholder to the table and describes it as a real high and low point:

Talking about pedagogy was very difficult. Providing an environment where teachers were able to open up about their challenges in the classroom and to ask for advice and support from peers requires vulnerability, and it takes a lot of time to establish trust.

She created protocols for the conversations, made clear agendas for the meetings, and began the slow process of helping the team through the predictable stages of team development. It took her years. Sometimes the conversation would get bogged down in topics that didn't have anything to do with pedagogical change, like lunch duty, but Sandra adapted as needed: "Sometimes if people want to talk about lunch duty, you have to keep both going; be flexible, keep the conversation moving forward."

Reflecting back on her tenure, Sandra notes that it takes more time than we think and that leading change and building teams requires the long-term view:

> My first two years as principal involved listening and asking lots of questions. Years three and four were a time of creation, a time of wonder, and a time for team building. During years five through seven, I felt like everyone was on board and rowing together. The teams still had to work at it, it wasn't automatic, but there was a real sense of joy with the teaching and learning for students and adults alike.

Building teams takes time, but it is the oil in the gears in the shift from the industrial model of education to a postindustrial system of learning. Figure 4.6 is a reference guide on how to help move your team through those stages of team formation. It is grounded in Bruce Tuckman's (1965) work on the developmental sequence of small groups. Tuckman defines the stages of team development as "forming" (the honeymoon period), "storming" (when reality hits and conflict emerges), "norming" (building the skills to engage in productive conflict with agreed-upon norms of behavior), and "performing" (full responsibility of team working toward shared purpose). It takes time to build and sustain teams and there are many resources out there that are helpful as teams work through the stages of forming, storming, norming, and performing. The reference guide on the next page will be a helpful resource for the team and its team leader to understand the tasks needed to move from one stage to the next.

Strategy 7: It Could Be a Library or . . .

Purpose: Rethink and reimagine the use of resources to align with your pedagogical and curricular vision.

Resources:

Edutopia—search learning environment and spaces examples

The Third Teacher by OWP/P Architects, VS Furniture, & Bruce Mau Design (2010)

The Design Thinking for Educators Toolkit (IDEO, n.d.)

Figure 4.6 • The Four Stages of Team Development

	Feelings and Attitudes	Behaviors	Tasks
Forming	• The Honeymoon phase—team members are feeling happy to be part of the team • Members experience varying levels of commitment • Purpose of work is unclear • Some anxiety regarding future performance	• Many questions asked regarding expectations and role • "Polite" conversation • Communication is limited—often one or two team members dominate	• Build a clear purpose and direction for the team's work • Discuss how the purpose will be achieved (process) • Clarify team member roles • Discuss and clarify expectations • Discuss and establish ground rules and norms for team meetings • Get to know each other as people
Storming	• Feelings of disappointment and frustration with how things are progressing so far • Doubts regarding own and others' abilities • Disillusionment with team members, self, process	• Disagreement about roles, goals, process being expressed openly and/or behind closed doors • Criticism of team goals and process • Finger pointing and/or avoidance of difficult conversations • Previously agreed-upon ground rules or norms for team meetings are violated	• Review the team goals—do they need to be amended? • Review team member roles—do they need to be amended? • Develop team members' ability to raise and work through difficult issues by revisiting ground rules or team norms and how these will be used • Assess and test resource needs
Norming	• Increased feeling of safety in sharing opinions and views • Greater feeling of acceptance of differing points of view • Feeling the beginning of a sense of momentum	• Explicit use of ground rules or team norms to support meaningful conversation • Team members exhibit a shared sense of responsibility in achieving the team goal • Differing opinions are shared openly and constructively	• Conduct regular check-ins regarding team process and progress against goals • Build relevant feedback loops with stakeholders • Develop methods and process to share information, resources, just-in-time feedback
Performing	• Sense of accomplishment and forward momentum • A feeling of "We can do this" shared by team members	• Full responsibility taken by all team members for team process and outcomes • Problems are addressed before they become major issues • Individual team members' strengths and differences are valued and used to help achieve goals	• Work continuously on team task and team relationships • Goals are measured against progress achieved • Continuously seek great practice • Celebrate progress along the way

Source: Table adapted from Tuckman (1965) and Stein (n.d.).

The constraints of the school schedule and how space is traditionally used can become obstacles or pathways to seeing your pedagogical and curricular vision realized. The example I shared earlier of Revere High School (RHS) and its schedule change allows every single teacher to participate in a Professional Learning Group during school hours and a much more in-depth advisory opportunity for students. In addition to the schedule change, RHS reconceived the notion of a traditional library and created the Learning Commons. It was designed as "an innovative learning environment that promotes active learning, critical thinking, collaborative learning, and knowledge building." It is a comfortable, flexible, welcoming environment with lots of different spaces for the community to collaborate, meet, and host special events. It has its own "Genius Bar" for Tech support for the 1:1 iPad program and is the home of the student internship program and the student-led Writing Center and, of course, a cozy reading nook for reading or quiet study.

Exercise: Convene Design Team(s) to Reconfigure Your Learning Environment

The configuration of the learning environment can be a powerful support or impediment to the learning process, and there are many incredible examples out there from no-cost to high-cost options (see *The Third Teacher* [OWP/P Architects et al., 2010] or search Edutopia for inspirational examples). Once you have articulated the pedagogical and curricular vision for your school or district, gather a couple of design teams to brainstorm low- or no-cost options to reconfigure the use of time and space to support the vision. The Design Thinking for Educators Toolkit is a great resource by IDEO (n.d.) and Riverdale Country School and is available for free download at design thinkingforeducators.com.

Strategy 8: Measuring What We Value

Purpose: Begin the process of measuring the skills, knowledge, and habits of mind articulated in your school or district's North Star.

Resources:

> The Mastery Transcript Consortium
>
> Next Generation Learning Challenges (2017b), *NGLC Assessment for Learning Project*
>
> *Assessing the Learning That Matters Most* Report (Wilson, 2015)
>
> Leading Assessment Best Practices—Open Source Database

In Chapter 3, I shared the Crossing the Chasm model and showed how assessment can be a significant driver of systemwide change. Redesigning your school or district's assessment practices to measure what the school values is an integral part of realizing the school's pedagogical vision.

I encourage you to immerse yourself in this growing field—a field that is being built by and for educators. Here are a few resources to help you get started:

> **The Mastery Transcript Consortium (MTC, n.d.)**—The mission of the Mastery Transcript Consortium is to "create a high school transcript that transforms high school." Launched in 2017, and as of this writing, the consortium comprises over one hundred independent schools. The goal is to use the collective influence of independent schools to change the college admissions process—to ultimately impact the college preparation process for *all* schools (public and private) once proof of concept has been established.
>
> The MTC has the potential to measure what we say we truly value and to help high school graduates demonstrate their knowledge, skills, and habits of mind in a much more meaningful and demonstrable way. Follow the MTC work on Twitter @MastTranscript and check out the free resources on their website at http://www.mastery .org/resources.
>
> **Next Generation Learning Challenges (2002b), NGLC Assessment for Learning Project**—NGLC has been leading great work in funding and supporting existing schools and new school models that break away from the industrial mold. In 2015, having identified assessment as a key lever for systemic change, NGLC launched the "Assessment for Learning Project" grant as a means to help grow the nascent field. Interestingly, they eschewed the traditional Request for Proposal (RFP) approach and instead issued a Request for Learning (RFL), making it explicit that one of the key objectives of the grant is to help build and support promising practice. Twelve grants were awarded and I am hopeful we will start to see some of that work made public soon. In the meantime, follow their work via Twitter @ALPinsights and at https://www.assessmentforlearningproject.org.
>
> **Assessing the Learning That Matters Most**—Many schools across the country are already building their own meaningful assessments and leading the way in measuring what they value. In 2015, I conducted a research project to inventory leading assessment practices, identify gaps, and highlight exemplary practices. Twenty-eight experts gave generously of their time and insights. You can access a free copy of the report *Assessing the Learning That Matters Most* at http://www.the-IFL.org/blog/2015/10/31/assessing-the-learning-that-matters-most. In addition, the research provided the foundation to build a beta version of an open source database of leading

assessment practices, including rubrics, protocols, and sample lesson plans. The items are categorized in the database as follows: Creativity, Collaboration, Communication, Critical Thinking, Social Emotional Learning, Grade Level, Subject, and School Location. You can access a beta version of the database at http://www.ifldb .org/database-all.

When leading your organization through change, the bulk of your work is not only leading people through ambiguity, uncertainty, and fear, but also developing their individual capacity as leaders in the process. I once heard a coach say that "leaders don't create followers, leaders create leaders." The backdrop of so much of this work is the fundamental shift from a system of compliance, control, and mitigating risk, to one of autonomy, creativity, and embracing risk. This is not a small shift. It is a 180-degree change. In the same way that a master teacher does not convey knowledge, but rather designs and nurtures the conditions for deep learning to take place, as the leader, you are not simply conveying the change to be made and telling people to get on with it. Instead, you are designing and nurturing the conditions for the whole organization to learn through this process of change. You are helping everyone in your school become a leader of self and of others, as they shift from a compliance mindset to that of a creator.

And this brings me to your own development as a leader.

Key Points

The strategies in this chapter are grounded in the five success factors referenced in Chapter 3. They include real-life examples of how others have used these strategies where applicable and provide additional background and resources to help contextualize some of the concepts discussed. Here is a high-level summary of the strategies:

1. Your Learning History

    Purpose: Provide a strong foundation for visioning work and collaboration by grounding the school and its community in the school's history and learning so far.

2. The Future: Where Would You Like to Go?

    Purpose: Generate a vision that begins the process of change in a sustainable, meaningful, and human-centered way.

3. Building Organizational Change Capacity

    Purpose: Identify priorities to begin the process of building organizational change capacity.

4. Helping Others Through Change—The Power of Development

   Purpose: Begin the process of developing people through change.

5. It's a Marathon, Not a Sprint—Leading Through the Uncertainty of Change

   Purpose: Understand the distinction between change and transition and help others through ambiguity and uncertainty.

6. Building Effective Teams

   Purpose: Set teams up for success by understanding the predictable stages of development and working on the tasks required at each stage.

7. It Could Be a Library or . . .

   Purpose: Rethink and reimagine the use of resources to align with your pedagogical and curricular vision.

8. Measuring What We Value

   Purpose: Begin the process of measuring the skills, knowledge, and habits of mind articulated in your school or district's North Star.

Questions for Reflection and Action

- How might you develop your teachers and administrators through the process of change?

- Which of the tools, strategies, and resources resonated with you?

- How and when will you implement them?

- What additional questions did this chapter prompt for you?

- What action items did this chapter prompt for you?

Notes

_____

_____

_____

_____

_____

_____

_____

_____

_____

_____

_____

_____

_____

_____

_____

_____

_____

_____

_____

_____

_____

_____

_____

_____

_____

CHAPTER 4

" You have a
masterpiece inside you,
you know. One unlike
any that has ever been
created, or ever will be.
If you go to your grave
without painting your
masterpiece, it will not
get painted. No one else
can paint it. Only you. "

—GORDON MACKENZIE,
ORBITING THE GIANT HAIRBALL

Chapter 5

LEADING YOURSELF THROUGH CHANGE

When You Are or Are Not in Charge

In 2015, I conducted a research report for Arthur Levine at the Woodrow Wilson Foundation titled *The K–12 Transformational Landscape*. The scope of the research was to interview a number of thought leaders to gain perspective on the short-, medium-, and long-term trends in the American K–12 education system, its primary challenges, and the biggest potential levers for change.

One of my biggest takeaways from the research was the growing sense of a bifurcating path and what might happen if we decide to stay on the path of the one-size-fits-all model, or make the choice to fundamentally rethink and reimagine the system.

Conducting the research helped me understand the terrain and the choices before us. Yes, there is much innovation happening. There is an ed tech bubble happening right now. There is the semblance of schools moving into the 21st century with iPads and apps and big data. But scratch under the surface, and a significant percentage of this "innovation" is simply technologizing the traditional system. Any technology that helps facilitate the processes and procedures existing in the current system is a much easier sell than something that will disrupt the status quo and support a more creative—and risky—approach.

What might happen if we double down on the industrial-era model with the power of technology?

The dystopian view is that we have millions of children isolated in front of computers or tablets being fed adaptive instruction. Students will progress in a linear way through a prescribed curriculum with little or no opportunity to create or think for themselves. Don't get me wrong, I have nothing against computer adaptive instruction; it is a helpful tool in the overall learning process. But if we do not stop to think about the overarching outcomes that we seek, then the default path is one of consumption, increasing isolation of the student, and reduced risk taking—aided, and made more efficient by, technology.

Conducting the research made me realize that the overall pace of change is too slow and that too many innovations, in particular technology innovations, are not actually that innovative. A deeper change is needed and technology (alone) is not our savior.

After I completed the research, I took an inventory of what I had learned after a decade of this work:

> We are asking a system designed on the principles of control, compliance, and consumption to change to its opposite, that is, a system of agency, autonomy, and creativity. It usually takes anywhere from five to seven years for a principal or superintendent to lead and implement this level of sustainable change.

> A new learning ecosystem is taking form and shape. The default of that shape could become a technologized version of the industrial model because our collective narrative of what "school" looks like is so strong.

> A potential reality is that the gap between the haves and have-nots widens further—a situation in which children of upper-middle-class parents have access to a wide array of choices, both online and offline, and build the skills and habits of mind that will enable them to thrive in our complex and ambiguous world—with a bare-bones, accountability-driven curriculum for children from the lower-middle-classes and in poverty.

> If we are serious about real change, we need to start asking ourselves, "What needs to end?" We do a very poor job of taking things off the plate of education. We just keep adding more. What should the education system stop doing? When was the last time federal- and state-level education policies were reviewed with a view to which policies support what we want to see and which ones do not?

Why am I sharing this? Because there are days when I am overwhelmed by the magnitude of the task before us. There are days when I tell myself I should stop trying to change an obsolete system that will never change in a meaningful way. It was not designed to change. I should just focus on helping to build the new learning ecosystem and stop trying to change a century-plus-old bureaucracy.

But then there are days when I see a team of teachers design a class together and I can see that each person on that team is playing in their zone of genius. There are days when I see a principal be vulnerable in front of his community when he describes the North Star and tells the group of assembled adults that he does not have all the answers and that he needs their help, and I see a community rally behind the change with head and heart. There are days like the day when I walked through the hallways of Columbus Signature Academy and saw fourteen-year-old students mastering the skills it took me well into my early thirties to learn.

And it is on those days when I know this level of change is possible and when I double down on its purpose.

I was raised in the old system. Perhaps you were too—a system of compliance, consumption, and control. The irony is that many of us in the current system were successful in the old, and here we are knowing that it needs to change and that we do not have all the answers. The right answer no longer resides at the back of the textbook.

It resides within us.

It resides in our individual and collective will to embrace ambiguity, uncertainty, and risk, to hold the vision steady and to work toward it with steadfast commitment and an understanding that it takes time. It takes time, patience, and heart.

It resides in our ability to break free of the double binds of "learned helplessness" and "waiting for permission" that the system too often perpetuates.

And this brings me to you.

What is the change that you want to see?

You do not need a formal position of power or authority (such as principal or superintendent) to lead change in the education system. The reality is we need hundreds of thousands of change agents, working both inside and outside the system, if we are to see sustainable and meaningful change in this next decade. We need change agents at all levels.

You might be a principal or superintendent who has a vision like Sandra Trach or David Miyashiro and who wants to see the untapped potential of students and teachers unleashed in pursuit of a more meaningful education.

You might be a concerned citizen with an idea for a program that you know will help teenagers in your community to bring back their love of learning and pride in themselves and their abilities.

You might be a parent, not liking the local options for your children, and wanting to build something different.

You might be a teacher who works in a school where the industrial model is still the accepted norm, but you know there is a better way for you to teach and you are committed to building your craft.

You might be a policymaker who wants to sunset those educational policies that no longer serve our children.

You might be an entrepreneur with an idea that bypasses the system entirely and that has the capacity to reach thousands of children.

Regardless of the change you want to see, the more change leaders I coach, the more I see that every single one of them is on the path of the Hero's Journey.

The Hero's Journey

"What is the change you want to see and what is your first step?"

Your answer to this question puts you on your own personal path of change.

In 2012, I was invited to speak at a TEDx event in Washington, DC. The theme for the event was "The Hero's Journey." I had not heard of the Hero's Journey before and began to learn more about its structure as a narrative tool. I learned that Joseph Campbell was one of the leading researchers and writers on the "monomyth" and how the Hero's Journey is a universal guide for the explorer setting out on an unknown journey and the joys and trials that he or she will find on the path.

As I learned more about the Hero's Journey, I began to see its application to the education system and to the children within it. During that TEDx talk, I spoke about the great work I was seeing in schools across the country and I gave the talk the title "Every Hero Has to Find Their Own Way." My intent with the title was to underscore that each student is a hero and has to find his or her own way—and a generative learning environment provides that.

I have come to realize that the same thing applies to us, the people who want to see change in the education system. If there is change that you want you see, you are being called to live the change that you seek.

At its core, the Hero's Journey is a journey from what you know to what you do not know, from the known world to the unknown world (see Figure 5.1). This is exciting and scary in equal measure. It takes us to the edge of our comfort zone and what we know. It requires us to embrace uncertainty, risk, and adventure.

Figure 5.1 • The Hero's Journey

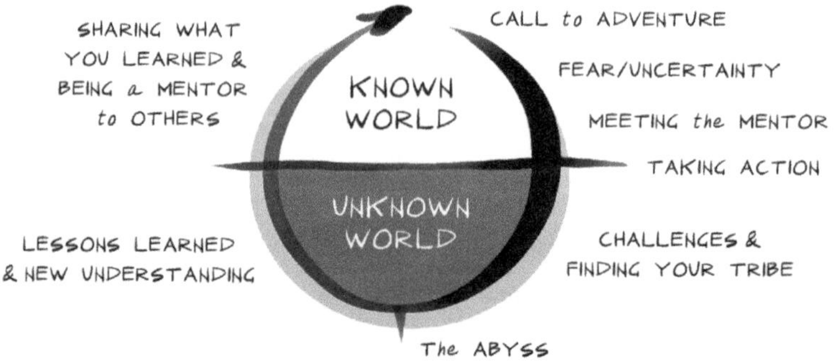

Source: Adapted from Campbell (1973). Illustration by Kelvy Bird.

CHAPTER 5

Stages of the Hero's Journey

1. **Call to Adventure.** The Call to Adventure can be an external event, a challenge, an opportunity, an idea, or an internal shift. You have been living in your ordinary world, but now things feel different—there is something inside you that is calling you to adventure and to leave the current and known world behind. You might be a teacher with an idea for an app, a new principal with a different vision for your school, or a parent who is frustrated with the limited education options available to your child.

2. **Fear and Uncertainty.** Having heard the Call to Adventure, you begin to feel the uncertainty and fear of embracing the unknown. You know the path is uncertain and full of risks, and you don't (yet) have the skills for the task at hand. As a teacher, you might tell yourself you do not know much about technology, so how can you start to build an app? As a new principal, you might doubt that anybody else in the community shares your vision. As a parent, you might be overwhelmed at the thought of what it takes to launch a new school.

3. **Meeting the Mentor.** Serendipitously, you meet the mentor. Meeting the mentor can be listening to your own inner voice, or it can be meeting a wise friend, colleague, or stranger who helps you with advice and support for the journey ahead. You might find that mentor inside or outside of your school context; they may be outside the education system entirely.

4. **Taking Action.** You commit to the path and cross the threshold from your known (and in many ways, safe) world to the unknown world. You decide to attend the weekend hackathon to build a prototype of your app, you invite the community into a conversation about the vision for your school, or you host a meeting of like-minded parents who are dissatisfied with their local school options.

5. **Challenges and Finding Your Tribe.** Having crossed the threshold, you meet a series of challenges, allies, and enemies. Sometimes those enemies are external. Sometimes they take the form of your inner critic, telling you that you are not capable of what you have chosen to take on—that it is too big, too scary, and who do you think you are for even trying? It is also a time when you meet people who are on a similar path, who resonate deeply with your work or goal. These are the people who offer commitment, support, and help when your perseverance and commitment are tested. They are your adventure-sustaining tribe.

6. **The Abyss.** There comes a stage on your journey when you meet that which you fear the most. It can feel like a life or death experience. It puts you through the wringer and you are not sure if you are going to get through it. You go into this darkest of caves

and you leave the old version of you behind when you walk out. Perhaps as a teacher, you are confronted with your fear that you do not have what it takes to be an entrepreneur; as a principal, you learn that you were third choice for the principal position and feel like you are crumbling under the weight of what you have taken on; as a parent, you find yourself enmeshed in regulation after regulation and can no longer see a way to changing the options for your child.

7. **Lessons Learned and New Understanding.** This is the treasure that was found in that cave. Having faced death in its metaphorical sense, you have discovered a gift or a newfound understanding. That gift or new understanding is now an integral part of who you are. As that teacher, you discovered that you *do* have what it takes; it is not some magical entrepreneurial gift, but rather tenacity and stubbornness that is needed—and you have an abundance of both qualities. As the new principal, you let go of your vision and needing it to be perfect and begin to see the community rally around changes that are meaningful to them; as the parent, you realize you cannot do this alone and begin reaching out to many more people to help.

8. **Sharing What You Learned and Being a Mentor to Others.** You are transformed by this journey and return to the world you once knew, sharing what you have learned. You inspire and help others with your mastery and mentor others on the path. As an entrepreneurial teacher, you mentor other teachers who have ideas they want to develop and inspire them with your story; as the principal, you mentor other principals on what it takes to lead meaningful change; as the parent, you share your experience with others to begin to change state policy.

The Hero's Journey of Real People Like You

"Yesterday I was clever, so I wanted to change the world. Today I am wise, so I am changing myself."

—Rumi

Over the years, I have met many heroes—visionary men and women working to transform the system. Some lead change from a position of formal power such as principal or superintendent; others do so informally as a teacher, parent, student, policymaker, entrepreneur, or concerned citizen. Some work within the system and others from outside it.

Their stories provide examples of what the Hero's Journey looks like in action and how each person's experience, while unique, follows a predictable cadence and path.

For example, Allison Ohle is a wife, mother, teacher, and leader. Her story is an example of how the work that is in our hearts to do can come in interesting packages and how choices are seldom clear cut or easy on the hero's path.

Allison was a founding teacher at a KIPP (Knowledge is Power Program) school in Oakland, California, in the early 2000s. She loved the mission and the work was incredibly rewarding. At the same time, the workload was enormous. "It was old-school KIPP; it was tough love and the pace of work was exhausting."

When she found out she was pregnant with her first child, she knew she couldn't maintain that pace and give it her all. So she went to Harvard's Kennedy School to study for a master's in public policy. Allison notes, "It says a lot about the pace of work at KIPP at that time that it was more feasible for me to move cross country, with an infant, and study full-time at Harvard, than to teach there."

Melissa Corto is teacher turned entrepreneur. Melissa's story shows us what is possible when a teacher sees a need and takes the steps necessary to meet that need, even if it lies outside her job description, comfort zone, and the place she calls home. As a special education teacher in Brooklyn, New York, Melissa constantly felt like she was failing to meet the standards and give the kids what they needed.

It was impossible to feel successful. If I was being successful with the kids, I was not meeting "the standards" as determined by the state. If I focused on the standards, I knew I was leaving the kids behind. There was always a mismatch of where the curriculum expected us to be in terms of testing and where the kids actually were in terms of their learning and what I felt they needed.

Zach Eikenberry's journey began as a young college graduate, living a life of fun singledom in Indianapolis, Indiana. The next four years would see him move from Indianapolis, build a school in Greenville, South Carolina, and undergo a life-changing personal transformation in the process. Zach's story is an example of what is possible when you dream big, fail, and keep taking the steps necessary to turn your dream into reality.

Natalie Belli is a fifth-grade teacher in Marblehead, Massachusetts. Natalie's Hero's Journey is an inspirational story of how your calling never leaves you. It might reside in the background for years, but it is always there; and when you take the steps to answer that call to adventure, the people and the resources begin to appear. Natalie's story is also a story that shows us what is possible within the confines of the current system. Where some see constraints and powerlessness, Natalie sees freedom and the power to create.

The golden thread of the Hero's Journey runs through Allison's, Melissa's, Zach's, and Natalie's story. Although they are driven by different reasons to transform our education system, the narrative arc of their path reflects the eight stages of the Hero's Journey. These stages are predictable and provide a practical tool for reflection, growth, and sense making of your own journey in this work. You might be a young twentysomething like Zach, a thirtysomething like Melissa, or more advanced in your career like

Allison and Natalie; regardless, at any point in your journey, you have the opportunity to embrace your own Hero's Journey.

The Call to Adventure can arise in many forms. For Zach, it was the death of a close friend at 23. He was forever changed in that moment and called to do something different with his life. As Allison was learning as much as she could about education and public policy at Harvard and subsequently working at a leading school (High Tech High), KIPP was always in the background—until she was ready for the call to lead an emerging region of KIPP schools. Melissa worked for nine years teaching students with special needs, during which time, she was not only teaching full time, but also building an online tool that would help teachers differentiate instruction. Sometimes we hear the call but are persuaded by ourselves or others to ignore it. That was the case for Natalie. She knew after a writing course in high school that she wanted to be a teacher, but her writing professor discouraged her from that path and Natalie subsequently ignored the call for decades.

Each of these heroes experienced fear, uncertainty, and doubt on their path. Melissa thought she needed an MBA to launch a business, and Zach was very aware that he did not know the world of education reform as he built a new school from scratch. Allison had very mixed feelings about going back to KIPP, and Natalie's writing professor unwittingly prompted her to turn away from her calling for decades.

Meeting the Mentor proved pivotal for each of our heroes. A conversation with an ex-colleague and mentor, Peter Bencivenga, gave Melissa the courage to take her idea and to run with it. A creative and visionary district colleague, Beth Delforge, showed Natalie what was possible in a public school classroom and lit a fire within her to do the work that she was being called to do. Allison's friend helped her work through her mixed feelings in going back to KIPP, and Ed Combs was the steady head and heart that helped Zach gain community support for a very different kind of high school in Greenville, South Carolina.

Having committed to the path, each person is tested. We meet the edge of what we know and that of which we are capable. It is also a time of finding and meeting your fellow tribe members and leaning on them when things get difficult. We are tested by what we know and what we do not know. If you are on your Hero's Journey, by definition you have gone from the known to the unknown world. You do not (yet) have the skills, knowledge, and mindset to do the work. The beauty and the pain of the Hero's Journey is that you will build the skills and knowledge as you go, not before you start, and as long as you stay on your path.

And then comes the stage where you meet that which you feared the most. For many people, it can feel like an abyss, like entering a dark cave. While there are many mentors and allies on the Hero's Journey, you enter that cave alone. It is time to lead yourself. This is not to say that your tribe will not be there to help you; they will. But there is something that you need to go through that will galvanize you. There is some part of yourself that you need to leave behind in that cave and a new part of you that needs to emerge.

In Zach's case, after a two-week honeymoon period, the school he had worked so hard to build was on life support. The school's finances had not come through as anticipated, enrollment was down, and there was an embarrassing little amount of education happening. Everything was hitting at once—a student was caught with prescription drugs, teachers were not coming into work on time, other teachers were covering for those late teachers, he was unable to meet payroll, and community leaders were distancing themselves from him and from the school.

One evening he collapsed in tears. He was at a complete loss with how he was going to get the school back on track. He realized that the only way he would be OK would be if he were willing to see the school fail. He could no longer maintain the idol and the illusion that the school had to live up to what he wanted it to be. Before he would have said, "I will never be a failure; this must succeed." But then he realized that he had to be OK for it to fail in order to move forward. On his path to success, he had to embrace failure—not embrace it, as in a mild experiment, but as in fully surrendering to it. He told himself, "It's OK for me to fail and fail miserably." With that realization came freedom; Zach experienced a surge of energy to get up and keep going.

For Zach, he needed to fully surrender to failure in order to succeed. Not just embrace failure (which has a happy sounding ring to it), but fully surrender to it and a completely unforeseeable outcome. For Allison, it was realizing she needed to support the new principal in completely turning that KIPP school around. She could not be the leader who told everybody it was OK and that there were just a few tweaks to be made.

There is another theme I have noticed when a hero enters the cave in leading change in education. The bottom is directly linked to the change the hero wants to see in the broader education system. You cannot lead the change you want to see in the education system without experiencing the full force of that desired change in your own life. What do I mean by that?

Zach's vision for the education system is that every child flourishes—and flourishes by having wrestled with and overcome his or her doubts and by embracing failure. He hit rock bottom weeks after the school opened; the school was failing on many levels. The only way out was for Zach to do that which he wants to see for our kids, that is, to fully surrender to the transformative power of unmitigated failure—and to learn from it. Allison works in education because she believes it is the most powerful tool for social justice. She needed to walk toward those mixed feelings of working for KIPP again and do the work in a school and in a community that needs it most. She believes in the transformative power of kids engaging in meaningful work—and she had to engage in her own meaningful work, and believe in her own capacity, to lead the change she wants to see in her own community and the broader KIPP network.

Having gone through the abyss and survived, heroes are transformed and share what they have learned with others. They become mentors. Melissa is now teaching children how to build and launch their own business. Zach has opened a second school and is mentoring the school principals in both schools. Allison is leading a revitalized team in providing a meaningful education for their students and community and sharing what she learned within the broader KIPP network. Natalie teaches educators how to build meaningful learning environments for all children.

When I coach education leaders, whether they are inside or outside the system, the Hero's Journey helps them make the decisions that will keep them moving forward on the path. It is also a helpful tool to identify missteps, cul de sacs, and wrong turns. Over the years, I have noticed a number of common ways in which we stumble most often on the path—and ways in which we might regain our footing:

Stumbling Blocks

Continually second-guessing yourself and rotating in and out of the call to adventure and fear and uncertainty. If you are stuck, reach out for help. In almost twenty years of coaching, I have yet to meet a single person who was able to cross the threshold from the safe known world to the unknown world without the help, guidance, or support from another person. It might be your spouse, colleague, a stranger, a child—regardless, they are instrumental in guiding you on your path and encouraging you to take the leap to the unknown.

Viewing challenges as evidence that you should give up. You are being tested. There is something to learn in every challenge, yet your inner critic can translate a challenge as "See? Told you it wouldn't work." Reflect on the challenges you have experienced so far. What did you learn? The good news is that there is something to learn in every challenge. The bad news is, if you do not learn it, it will repeat itself until you do—and the lessons become harder each time you ignore the learning.

Not reaching out for help. When you find yourself in an unknown world, there are a lot of new people for you to meet. There is a tribe of supporters, confidants, allies, and mentors waiting for you. You need them. And although you might not think it at the time, they need you too. Being on the Hero's Journey does not mean being a lone wolf. You will not see the change you want to see by walking this path alone. It takes the power of the individual AND the collective when you work at this level of change.

While the challenges and opportunities to stumble are plentiful on the Hero's Journey, the capacity for growth, learning, and self-discovery are equal in measure. It is a path of deep learning. It brings us up against the limit of our current knowledge, skills, and abilities—the very knowledge, skills, and abilities we learned via the old system. The vast majority of us who have an appetite and heart to change education were successful in the old system, and we find ourselves as the hospice workers to the old ways and midwives to the new (Leicester, 2013). By definition, this brings us to the edge of our skill set and invites us to learn the skills we want our kids to learn, that is, working collaboratively with others, solving problems, directing our own learning, and embracing risk and failure as an inherent part of learning and growth.

There are approximately 15,000 school districts in the United States, comprising approximately 15,000 superintendents and 115,000 principals. It is unlikely that every single one of these leaders, in a formal position of authority, will lead the kind of change we need in the next decade. Many are—there is incredible work happening, work that is highlighted by the 145 school districts represented in the EdLeader21 network, the twenty states represented by the Partnership for 21st Century Learning, and the five hundred schools in the Hewlett Deeper Learning network—AND we need more. We need more people doing the work that is in their heart to do. You do not need a formal position of authority to begin your own Hero's Journey in this work. All you need to do is to take your first step.

Key Points

- You do not need a formal position of power or authority to lead change in the education system.

- We need hundreds of thousands of change agents, working both inside and outside the system, if we are to see sustainable and meaningful change in this next decade.

- When you are leading change, you are on a Hero's Journey.

- The Hero's Journey is a journey from what you know to what you don't know, from the known world to the unknown world. The stages of the Hero's Journey are

  o Call to Adventure

  o Fear and Uncertainty

  o Meeting the Mentor

  o Taking Action

  o Challenges and Finding Your Tribe

- o The Abyss
- o Lessons Learned and New Understanding
- o Sharing What You Learned and Being a Mentor to Others
- You do not need a formal position of authority to begin your own Hero's Journey in this work. All you need to do is to take your first step.

Questions for Reflection and Action
Your Hero's Journey

Call to Adventure: What is calling you? What are you becoming more aware of? What is the change you would like to see? Why is this change important to you?

Fear and Uncertainty: What fears come up for you when you think about this change? What is uncertain about this change? What are the "unknowns"? What will happen if the change does not happen?

Meeting the Mentor: Who might help you on your journey? Who could be part of your tribe? How might they help you? Is there a group of like-minded people out there, who share your purpose and passion, with whom you could join? Is this an opportunity to build a new tribe from scratch? How might you be your own mentor?

Taking Action: It's time to take action—and it does not have to be a massive leap, unless you want it to be. It can be a small step. What's the small action step you could take *today* to move your vision forward?

Challenges and Finding Your Tribe: Who is with you? Who is resisting the change? What challenges are you experiencing? What are you learning from those challenges? How might you align with your allies to help you weather that which your enemies throw at you? Sometimes your enemies are external, and sometimes they are internal—in the form of the inner critic.

The Abyss: What are your deepest fears in this work? How are you overcoming them? What is the biggest lesson that you are here to learn through this work? Why is this lesson important? What parts of yourself do you have to let go of? What part of you needs to die, in order to move on?

Lessons Learned and New Understanding: What are the lessons learned? What new thing about yourself do you need to claim? How are you fortified to do the work that is in your heart to do? Having gone through the previous stages of the Hero's Journey, how are you changed?

Sharing What You Learned and Being a Mentor to Others: How can your story help others? How can your work have a broader impact beyond yourself or beyond your own school or community? How can you communicate your story and your work to the larger community?

Notes

" If you can't fly then run, if you can't run then walk, if you can't walk then crawl, but whatever you do you have to keep moving forward. **"**

—MARTIN LUTHER KING, JR.

Conclusion

In 2009, Simon Sinek gave a TEDx talk titled "How Great Leaders Inspire Action." My favorite quote from Simon's talk is "People don't buy what you do; they buy why you do it."

If we are serious about seeing real change in the education system in this lifetime, we need an army of changemakers who have gotten really clear on their *why*, live it, and share it with as many people as possible as they chart their own Hero's Journey.

That's my *what*. Here's my *why*.

I have worked with thousands of adults over two decades. I see the results of an industrial system of education. I see adults who graduated the system "successfully" yet who do not have the skills and knowledge to design and build a life of their own choosing. The pace of change is accelerating and the gap between the haves and have-nots is widening. I believe in the American Dream. I moved to this country as a twenty-two-year-old in pursuit of it. I want every child to have the opportunity to build and design a life of their own choosing, regardless of demography. I believe twelve years in a system of education should provide that opportunity. I know that adults are the key to making this change for our children. I work with burned out educators, overwhelmed administrators, and anxious parents. The education system has lost its heart. We need to bring back that heart. Why? Because heart is at the core of education. Heart is at the core of change. Heart is where learning and change are possible.

Getting Clear on Your "Why" and Taking Action

Why do you do the work that you do? Once you ground in your *why*, it becomes your call to action. Embarking on the Hero's Journey, and staying on your path, is one of the most challenging things you will do. But there is one thing that I have seen that will hold you. It will hold you when you meet your demons, the naysayers, and the edge of what you know and are capable of. It's your *why*. Why you are doing this work is your personal North Star and it speaks to your legacy—the final stage of the Hero's Journey. Your *why* has a dual purpose: It keeps you focused on your path and is an inspiration to others.

So what is your *why*? What is the personal legacy you would like to leave?

Write it down, live it, and share it with others. We need you to do the work that is in your heart to do. If you share the vision I outlined in the first part of this book, and if you have an idea to make it a reality, ground yourself in your *why* and take the first step. When you take that first step, you are on your path, and when you are on your path, you are following your own curriculum.

In writing this book, I wanted to highlight the major tasks of human-centered change as I see them and to provide examples, tools, strategies, and resources along the way. Take what is helpful and disregard that which is not. The reality of being a change leader in this work is that your path is unique to you. There is no fail-safe manual that will get you from here to there. We must stop trying to change the education system with "guaranteed outcomes" and outdated linear theories of change.

> "If you find your path laid out in front of you step by step, you know it's not your path. Your own path you make with every step you take. That's why it's your path."
>
> —Joseph Campbell

Be a learner, embrace the lessons, and walk your own path of change and transformation. The extent to which our education system changes in the next decade is directly proportional to the extent to which we, the adults, change in that same timeframe. We need you to lead yourself and others through this change. You have a unique set of talents and a unique purpose. Ground yourself in both and lead yourself from that place.

Yes, there will be setbacks along the way. There will be days, weeks, and months when it feels like you are making no progress. It is to be expected. You are leading a change that is difficult. If it were easy, the change would have happened by now. But if you take the long-term view that, at its core, you are helping your school or district build change capacity, and you are developing others to lead and implement this work, then you will give yourself and others the time, patience, and heart to continue and see it through. The Five Success Factors I referenced are not the be-all and end-all of school change, but I do believe they comprise several major puzzle pieces, and if they are in place, the change stands a greater chance of being sustainable. Your situation is unique. Take the success factors as a starting point and build your own strategy of developmental change. As I mentioned several times, do not do this work alone—find your tribe. You need them and they need you.

If you are leading change outside the system, it is even more important to find your tribe and to lean on them. Embrace the possibility of your idea, find like-minded people, and take your first step. Yes, the idea might not work out; if it does not, what you learn will guide you to what is next. If it does work, keep on keeping on.

Changing our education system is not like changing a corporation. We should not judge our progress based on quarterly results. Changing the education system is generational work. It is the very definition of taking the long-term view. I think of it as growing bamboo. It takes approximately three to four years for a young bamboo plant to establish a large and solid root structure underground before it starts growing significantly above ground. It would appear that not a lot is happening for a long period of time. But, after three to four years of consistent watering and care, that very same plant can grow several feet overnight. This work of changing the education system is just like bamboo growth; it requires patience and time—and it also requires faith.

Know that your work matters and that we need you to do it. Follow your own inner compass toward the direction of your North Star and be open to the places and people where it leads you. May we all be part of not just a rising consensus of what needs to change, but also a rising army of hundreds of thousands of people doing something about it—with humility, with heart, and with faith.

Summary Questions for Reflection and Action

- What is the change you are leading?

- What is the problem this change is solving?

- What will happen if you do nothing?

- What will success look like when the change has been completed (for students, parents, teachers, administrators, community members)?

- What major challenges might you experience along the way?

- How will you address each of these challenges?

- Which strengths or talents will you use? How?

- How will you unleash talent and build teams around this change?

- How will you manage resistance?

- Describe the high-level plan of the change and a draft timeline.

- What are your big milestones along the way? How will you know when you have reached them?

- How will you sustain yourself as a leader of change throughout the process?

Appendix

Organizational Change Capacity Questionnaire

Part 1: Questions

Circle one number on each of the following 0 to 10 scales with reference to your school.

1. We place a strong emphasis on learning and information sharing.

0	1	2	3	4	5	6	7	8	9	10

   Never ———————————————— Sometimes ———————————————— Almost Always

2. We hold meetings across all grade levels that focus on identifying and critically assessing new curricular and pedagogical opportunities.

0	1	2	3	4	5	6	7	8	9	10

   Never ———————————————— Sometimes ———————————————— Almost Always

3. We use a common, schoolwide framework for thinking and communicating about change.

0	1	2	3	4	5	6	7	8	9	10

   Never ———————————————— Sometimes ———————————————— Almost Always

4. We communicate an enduring, shared purpose that is well understood by everyone in the school.

0	1	2	3	4	5	6	7	8	9	10

   Never ———————————————— Sometimes ———————————————— Almost Always

5. We designate and hold accountable an owner of the goal to develop our school's change capacity.

0	1	2	3	4	5	6	7	8	9	10

   Never ———————————————— Sometimes ———————————————— Almost Always

6. We select, hire, evaluate, and reward our employees based, in part, on their ability to thrive on change.

0	1	2	3	4	5	6	7	8	9	10

   Never ———————————————— Sometimes ———————————————— Almost Always

7. We encourage everyone in the school to ask questions and speak the truth, especially when people perceive problems or obstacles.

0	1	2	3	4	5	6	7	8	9	10

   Never ———————————————— Sometimes ———————————————— Almost Always

8. We conduct low-cost experiments with new ideas.

| 0 | 1 | 2 | 3 | 4 | 5 | 6 | 7 | 8 | 9 | 10 |

Never ———————————— Sometimes ———————————— Almost Always

9. The people in our school understand there are different approaches to change and when each is appropriate.

| 0 | 1 | 2 | 3 | 4 | 5 | 6 | 7 | 8 | 9 | 10 |

Never ———————————— Sometimes ———————————— Almost Always

10. We encourage people to think dynamically and systematically so that strategies can change quickly.

| 0 | 1 | 2 | 3 | 4 | 5 | 6 | 7 | 8 | 9 | 10 |

Never ———————————— Sometimes ———————————— Almost Always

11. We devote resources to scanning the external environment in search of new ideas for student learning.

| 0 | 1 | 2 | 3 | 4 | 5 | 6 | 7 | 8 | 9 | 10 |

Never ———————————— Sometimes ———————————— Almost Always

12. We create teams with maximum diversity to encourage innovation and creativity.

| 0 | 1 | 2 | 3 | 4 | 5 | 6 | 7 | 8 | 9 | 10 |

Never ———————————— Sometimes ———————————— Almost Always

13. We encourage everyone to empathize with and value alternative viewpoints.

| 0 | 1 | 2 | 3 | 4 | 5 | 6 | 7 | 8 | 9 | 10 |

Never ———————————— Sometimes ———————————— Almost Always

14. We recognize and reward people who support, encourage, lead, and share learning about organizational change.

| 0 | 1 | 2 | 3 | 4 | 5 | 6 | 7 | 8 | 9 | 10 |

Never ———————————— Sometimes ———————————— Almost Always

15. We focus on developing deep expertise about how to implement organizational change.

| 0 | 1 | 2 | 3 | 4 | 5 | 6 | 7 | 8 | 9 | 10 |

Never ———————————— Sometimes ———————————— Almost Always

16. We thoroughly examine the future of education, changing demographics, competitors, and organizational opportunities.

| 0 | 1 | 2 | 3 | 4 | 5 | 6 | 7 | 8 | 9 | 10 |

Never ———————————— Sometimes ———————————— Almost Always

17. We encourage our employees to get to know our students and their parent(s) or guardian(s).

| 0 | 1 | 2 | 3 | 4 | 5 | 6 | 7 | 8 | 9 | 10 |

Never ———————————— Sometimes ———————————— Almost Always

18. We develop, reward, and promote department heads and administrators who enable change.

0	1	2	3	4	5	6	7	8	9	10

Never ——————————————— Sometimes ——————————————— Almost Always

19. We support people who take risks and apply innovative ideas.

0	1	2	3	4	5	6	7	8	9	10

Never ——————————————— Sometimes ——————————————— Almost Always

20. We maintain a fluid organizational structure that allows the quick formation of new groups as needed.

0	1	2	3	4	5	6	7	8	9	10

Never ——————————————— Sometimes ——————————————— Almost Always

21. We provide change coaching and consulting services to our people and departments.

0	1	2	3	4	5	6	7	8	9	10

Never ——————————————— Sometimes ——————————————— Almost Always

22. We factor future scenarios into today's decisions.

0	1	2	3	4	5	6	7	8	9	10

Never ——————————————— Sometimes ——————————————— Almost Always

23. We appoint a committed change sponsor for each organizational change.

0	1	2	3	4	5	6	7	8	9	10

Never ——————————————— Sometimes ——————————————— Almost Always

24. We work hard to enhance the personal credibility of school leaders.

0	1	2	3	4	5	6	7	8	9	10

Never ——————————————— Sometimes ——————————————— Almost Always

25. We tolerate mistakes in the interest of learning.

0	1	2	3	4	5	6	7	8	9	10

Never ——————————————— Sometimes ——————————————— Almost Always

26. We create systems and processes for sharing knowledge, information, and learning across boundaries.

0	1	2	3	4	5	6	7	8	9	10

Never ——————————————— Sometimes ——————————————— Almost Always

27. We encourage the formation of change agent networks to share best practices, tools, and research about organizational change.

0	1	2	3	4	5	6	7	8	9	10

Never ——————————————— Sometimes ——————————————— Almost Always

28. We focus on stringing together an ongoing series of new student learning pilots.

| 0 | 1 | 2 | 3 | 4 | 5 | 6 | 7 | 8 | 9 | 10 |

Never ————————————————— Sometimes ————————————————— Almost Always

29. We provide key change projects with enough resources to get highly visible, public successes.

| 0 | 1 | 2 | 3 | 4 | 5 | 6 | 7 | 8 | 9 | 10 |

Never ————————————————— Sometimes ————————————————— Almost Always

30. We listen to, encourage, and reward mavericks and trailblazers.

| 0 | 1 | 2 | 3 | 4 | 5 | 6 | 7 | 8 | 9 | 10 |

Never ————————————————— Sometimes ————————————————— Almost Always

31. We value conflict and use it to achieve understanding and creativity.

| 0 | 1 | 2 | 3 | 4 | 5 | 6 | 7 | 8 | 9 | 10 |

Never ————————————————— Sometimes ————————————————— Almost Always

32. We provide responsive and proactive training and education in support of specific organizational changes.

| 0 | 1 | 2 | 3 | 4 | 5 | 6 | 7 | 8 | 9 | 10 |

Never ————————————————— Sometimes ————————————————— Almost Always

33. We debrief people after important organizational changes with a focus on learning from experience.

| 0 | 1 | 2 | 3 | 4 | 5 | 6 | 7 | 8 | 9 | 10 |

Never ————————————————— Sometimes ————————————————— Almost Always

34. We create and communicate a change-friendly identity both internally to our employees and externally to our parents and community.

| 0 | 1 | 2 | 3 | 4 | 5 | 6 | 7 | 8 | 9 | 10 |

Never ————————————————— Sometimes ————————————————— Almost Always

35. We shelter breakthrough ideas with their own budgets and people.

| 0 | 1 | 2 | 3 | 4 | 5 | 6 | 7 | 8 | 9 | 10 |

Never ————————————————— Sometimes ————————————————— Almost Always

36. We create a climate of trust, honesty, and transparency.

| 0 | 1 | 2 | 3 | 4 | 5 | 6 | 7 | 8 | 9 | 10 |

Never ————————————————— Sometimes ————————————————— Almost Always

Part 2: Scoring and Interpretation

1. Next to each item number below, record your rating from Part 1 of this questionnaire. After you have entered your rating for each question, calculate the average score for each dimension.

Item	Score	Item	Score	Item	Score
1.	_____	2.	_____	3.	_____
7.	_____	8.	_____	9.	_____
13.	_____	14.	_____	15.	_____
19.	_____	20.	_____	21.	_____
25.	_____	26.	_____	27.	_____
31.	_____	32.	_____	33.	_____
TOTAL =	_____	TOTAL =	_____	TOTAL =	_____
$\frac{\text{Total} =}{6}$	_____	$\frac{\text{Total} =}{6}$	_____	$\frac{\text{Total} =}{6}$	_____
Facilitative Culture		**Supportive Infrastructure**		**Different Change Approaches**	
Item	Score	Item	Score	Item	Score
4.	_____	5.	_____	6.	_____
10.	_____	11.	_____	12.	_____
16.	_____	17.	_____	18.	_____
22.	_____	23.	_____	24.	_____
28.	_____	29.	_____	30.	_____
34.	_____	35.	_____	36.	_____
TOTAL =	_____	TOTAL =	_____	TOTAL =	_____
$\frac{\text{Total} =}{6}$	_____	$\frac{\text{Total} =}{6}$	_____	$\frac{\text{Total} =}{6}$	_____
Ongoing Strategizing		**Sufficient Resources**		**Willingness and Ability to Change**	

2. Which of the six major dimensions of change capacity is highest? Why?

3. Which of the six major dimensions of change capacity is lowest? Why?

4. Which of the six major dimensions of change capacity should be your top improvement priority? What specifically could be done to increase change capacity along this dimension?

Source: Adapted with permission from Buono & Kerber (2009).

online resources ↗ Available for download at **www.the-IFL.org/TheHumanSide**

Individual Development Plan

"Leading Change" at _____ [School Name]

Describe the changes you would like to lead at _____ [School Name] in the year ahead:

What excites you about these changes?

What concerns you about these changes?

Why do these changes matter to you?

What are your development goals for the year ahead?

How will _____ [School Name] have changed when you have achieved these goals?

What specific tools or skills in change leadership will help you get there?

What strengths will you use to help you get there?

What support do you need from your colleagues?

How and when will you check your progress?

The Strengths-Based Conversation

What talents or strengths do you use regularly in your role?

How do those talents or strengths help you be more successful in your role?

What talents or strengths do you have that are underutilized?

How might you bring more of those talents or strengths to your work?

What might be your most valuable contribution to this team?

What support do you need from your manager and/or colleagues to bring more of your strengths to work?

References

Abel Palmieri, L. (2017, March 16). *5 qualities of prepared leaders in a project-based world*. Retrieved from http://www.gettingsmart.com/2017/03/5-qualities-prepared-leaders-project-based-world

Asia Society. (n.d.). *Center for global education*. Retrieved from http://asiasociety.org/education

Barrett, T. (2013). *Can computers keep secrets?: How a six-year-old's curiosity could change the world*. Edinburgh, Scotland: Notosh Publishing.

Bridges, W., & Bridges, S. (2017). *Managing transitions: Making the most of change*. London, England: Nicholas Brealey.

Buono, A. F., & Kerber, K. W. (2009). *Building organizational change capacity*. Paper presented at Management Consulting Division International Conference, Vienna, Austria.

Buono, A. F., & Kerber, K. W. (2010). Creating a sustainable approach to change: Building organizational change capacity. *S.A.M. Advanced Management Journal, Spring, 75*(2).

Campbell, J. (1973). *The hero with a thousand faces* (2nd ed.). Princeton, NJ: Princeton University Press.

Center for Advanced Research and Technology. (n.d.). Retrieved from http://cart.org

Conner, D. R. (2006). *Managing at the speed of change: How resilient managers succeed and prosper where others fail*. New York, NY: Random House.

Darling-Hammond, L., Ramos-Beban, N., Altamirano, R. P., & Hyler, M. E. (2016). *Be the change: Reinventing school for student success*. New York, NY: Teachers College Press.

Douglas County School District. (n.d.). *Douglas county school district strategic plan*. Retrieved from https://www.dcsdk12.org/district/strategic-plan

EdLeader21. (n.d.). *Profile of a graduate campaign*. Retrieved from http://profileofagraduate.org

Gallup. (n.d.). *Clifton strengths solutions*. Retrieved from https://www.gallupstrengthscenter.com/

Grove Consultants International. (n.d.). *Grove visual planning tools*. Retrieved from http://www.grove.com/products.php

Heifitz, R. A., Grashow, A., & Linsky, M. (2009). *The practice of adaptive leadership: Tools and tactics for changing your organization and the world*. Boston, MA: Harvard Business Press.

Hewlett Foundation. (2013, April). *Deeper learning competencies*. Retrieved from https://www.hewlett.org/wp-content/uploads/2016/08/Deeper_Learning_Defined__April_2013.pdf

IDEO. (n.d.). *Design thinking for educators*. Retrieved from https://designthinkingforeducators.com

Institute for the Future of Learning. (n.d.). *Open source database of emerging assessment practices*. Retrieved from http://www.ifldb.org/database-all

Kegan, R. (2003). *In over our heads: The mental demands of modern life*. Cambridge, MA: Harvard University Press.

Kotter, J. P. (2014). *Accelerate: Building strategic agility for a faster-moving world.* Boston, MA: Harvard Business Review Press.

Leicester, G. (2013, January 17). Road to radical change littered with obstacles. *The Scotsman.* Retrieved from https://www.scotsman.com/news/opinion/graham-leicester-road-to-radical-change-littered-with-obstacles-1-2741748

Lencioni, P. (2002a). *The five dysfunctions of a team: A leadership fable.* San Francisco, CA: Jossey-Bass.

Lencioni, P. (2002b). *The five dysfunctions of a team resources: Free tools and resources.* Retrieved from https://www.tablegroup.com/books/dysfunctions

MacKenzie, G. (1998). *Orbiting the giant hairball: A corporate's fool's guide to surviving with grace.* New York, NY: Viking.

Mastery Transcript Consortium. (n.d.). Retrieved October 10, 2017, from http://www.mastery.org

Mazur, E. (2007). *Confessions of a converted lecturer.* Retrieved from https://www.math.upenn.edu/~pemantle/active-papers/Mazurpubs_605.pdf

Meier, D. (2000). *The accelerated learning handbook: A creative guide to designing and delivering faster, more effective training programs.* New York, NY: McGraw Hill.

Moore, G. A. (2014). *Crossing the chasm: Marketing and selling disruptive products to mainstream customers.* New York, NY: HarperBusiness.

Mount Vernon Institute for Innovation. (2014, June). *DEEPdt design challenge playbook.* Atlanta, GA: Author.

Next Generation Learning Challenges. (2017a). *MyWays toolkit.* Retrieved from https://myways.nextgenlearning.org

Next Generation Learning Challenges. (2017b). *NGLC assessment for learning project.* Retrieved from https://nextgenlearning.org/grants/assessment-for-learning-project

OWP/P Architects, VS Furniture, & Bruce Mau Design. (2010). *The third teacher: 79 ways you can use design to transform teaching and learning.* New York, NY: Abrams.

Partnership for 21st Century Learning. (2017). *Framework for 21st century learning.* Retrieved from http://www.p21.org/our-work/p21-framework

Partnership for 21st Century Learning. (n.d.). *Our history.* Retrieved from http://www.p21.org/about-us/our-history

Perkins, D. (2006). *Educating for the unknown* [Course Syllabus]. Cambridge, MA: Harvard Graduate School of Education.

Rath, T., & Conchie, B. (2009). *Strengths based leadership: Great leaders, teams, and why people follow.* New York, NY: Gallup Press.

Robinson, K., & Aronica, L. (2016). *Creative schools: Revolutionizing education from the ground up.* London, England: Penguin Books.

Ryder, E. (2013, March 9). *I was creative, then I wasn't, now I am again: Journey of a PBL student.* Retrieved from https://newtechnetwork.org/resources/creative-wasnt-now-journey-pbl-student

School Retool. (n.d.). *Shadow a student challenge.* Retrieved from http://shadowastudent.org

Senge, P., Cambron-McCabe, N., Lucas, T., Smith, B., Dutton, J., & Kleiner, A. (2000). *Schools that learn: A fifth discipline fieldbook for educators, parents, and everyone who cares about education: Fifth discipline resource.* New York, NY: Doubleday.

Sinek, C. (2009). *How great leaders inspire action* [Video file]. Retrieved from https://www.ted.com/talks/simon_sinek_how_great_leaders_inspire_action

Stein, J. (n.d.). *Using the stages of team development*. Retrieved from http://hrweb.mit.edu/learning-development/learning-topics/teams/articles/stages-development

Tuckman, B. W. (1965). Developmental sequence in small groups. *Psychological Bulletin. 63*(6): 384–399

United Nations Educational, Scientific and Cultural Organization. (2015). *Global citizenship education: Topics and learning objectives* (Publication). Retrieved from http://unesdoc.unesco.org/images/0023/002329/232993e.pdf

VIA Institute on Character. (n.d.). VIA website. Retrieved from https://www.viacharacter.org

Wagner, T. (2014). *The global achievement gap: Why even our best schools don't teach the new survival skills our children need—and what we can do about it.* New York, NY: Basic Books.

Wilson, J. M. (2015, October). *Assessing the learning that matters most.* Retrieved from Institute for the Future of Learning website, http://www.the-ifl.org/blog/2015/10/31/assessing-the-learning-that-matters-most

World Economic Forum. (2016, January). *The 10 skills you need to thrive in the Fourth Industrial Revolution.* Retrieved from https://www.weforum.org/agenda/2016/01/the-10-skills-you-need-to-thrive-in-the-fourth-industrial-revolution

Index

what's worth learning? and, 71–72
See also Change agents;
    Organizational change
    strategies; Redesigned
    education systems; Successful
    change process
Volatile/uncertain/complex/
    ambiguous (VUCA) world, 9, 59

Wagner, T., 9, 11
What's worth learning?, 9
    consensus on, 9–12, 11 (figure)
    core competencies and,
        10, 11 (figure)
    human-centered change process
        and, 11
    postindustrial skills and, 11
    potential, unlocking of, xix, 3, 5, 7,
        10 (figure)
    soft skills and, 9
    survival skills and, 9, 10, 11 (figure)
    unlearning process and, 9, 11
    visioning process and, 71–72
    volatile/uncertain/complex/
        ambiguous world and, 9, 59
    worthy skills and, 9, 10 (figure)
    See also Instructional practices;
        Mastery learning;
        Postindustrial education
        model; Redesigned education

systems; Student learning;
    Worthy skills
Whole child approach, 56
Wilson, J. M., 85, 113, 114
Woodrow Wilson Foundation, 91
Workshop School, 56
World Economic Forum, 9
Worthy skills, 9, 10 (figure)
    collaborative learning and, 12
    creativity/innovation and, 15–17
    critical thinking/problem solving
        and, 25–26
    effective school leadership and,
        14–15, 18
    global citizenship and, 21–22
    interrelated/interdependent skills
        and, 12
    planning process, adaptability/
        agility in, 17–18
    questioning, emerging creativity
        and, 12–13
    relationship building and, 23–25
    self-directed learning and, 12–15
    self-efficacy and, 19–21
    strengths awareness/application
        and, 18–19
    See also Postindustrial education
        model; Redesigned education
        systems; What's worth
        learning?

CORWIN LEADERSHIP

Anthony Kim & Alexis Gonzales-Black
Designed to foster flexibility and continuous innovation, this resource expands cutting-edge management and organizational techniques to empower schools with the agility and responsiveness vital to their new environment.

Jonathan Eckert
Explore the collective and reflective approach to progress, process, and programs that will build conditions that lead to strong leadership and teaching, which will improve student outcomes.

PJ Caposey
Offering a fresh perspective on teacher evaluation, this book guides administrators to transform their school culture and evaluation process to improve teacher practice and, ultimately, student achievement.

Dwight L. Carter & Mark White
Through understanding the past and envisioning the future, the authors use practical exercises and real-life examples to draw the blueprint for adapting schools to the age of hyper-change.

Raymond L. Smith & Julie R. Smith
This solid, sustainable, and laser-sharp focus on instructional leadership strategies for coaching might just be your most impactful investment toward student achievement.

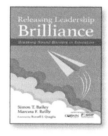

Simon T. Bailey & Marceta F. Reilly
This engaging resource provides a simple, sustainable framework that will help you move your school from mediocrity to brilliance.

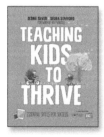

Debbie Silver & Dedra Stafford
Equip educators to develop resilient and mindful learners primed for academic growth and personal success.

Peter Gamwell & Jane Daly
Discover a new perspective on how to nurture creativity, innovation, leadership, and engagement.

To order your copies, visit **corwin.com/leadership**

Leadership That Makes an Impact

Steven Katz, Lisa Ain Dack, & John Malloy
Leverage the oppositional forces of top-down expectations and bottom-up experience to create an intelligent, responsive school.

Peter M. DeWitt
Centered on staff efficacy, these resources present discussion questions, vignettes, strategies, and action steps to improve school climate, leadership collaboration, and student growth.

Eric Sheninger
Harness digital resources to create a new school culture, increase communication and student engagement, facilitate real-time professional growth, and access new opportunities for your school.

Russell J. Quaglia, Kristine Fox, Deborah Young, Michael J. Corso, & Lisa L. Lande
Listen to your school's voice to see how you can increase engagement, involvement, and academic motivation.

Michael Fullan, Joanne Quinn, & Joanne McEachen
Learn the right drivers to mobilize complex, coherent, whole-system change and transform learning for all students.

CORWIN
A SAGE Publishing Company

Helping educators make the greatest impact

CORWIN HAS ONE MISSION: to enhance education through intentional professional learning.

We build long-term relationships with our authors, educators, clients, and associations who partner with us to develop and continuously improve the best evidence-based practices that establish and support lifelong learning.